THE USBORNE INTRODUCTION
TO THE
SECOND WORLD WAR

THE USBORNE INTRODUCTION
TO THE
SECOND WORLD WAR

Paul Dowswell

Designed by Leonard Le Rolland & Karen Tomlins

Edited by Jane Chisholm

Consultant: Terry Charman, Historian
Imperial War Museum

CONTENTS

THE DEFEAT OF JAPAN

THE WORLD AFTER THE WAR

These diagrams, drawn to help American pilots and anti-aircraft crews identify enemy planes, show the Japanese *Zero*, a fighter plane which played a major role in the attack on Pearl Harbor.

INTERNET LINKS

Throughout this book, we have recommended interesting websites where you can find out more about the Second World War and watch video clips, play games and view interactive exhibits. For links to the sites, go to the **Usborne Quicklinks Website** at **www.usborne-quicklinks.com** and enter the keywords "world war two".

How to use Usborne Quicklinks

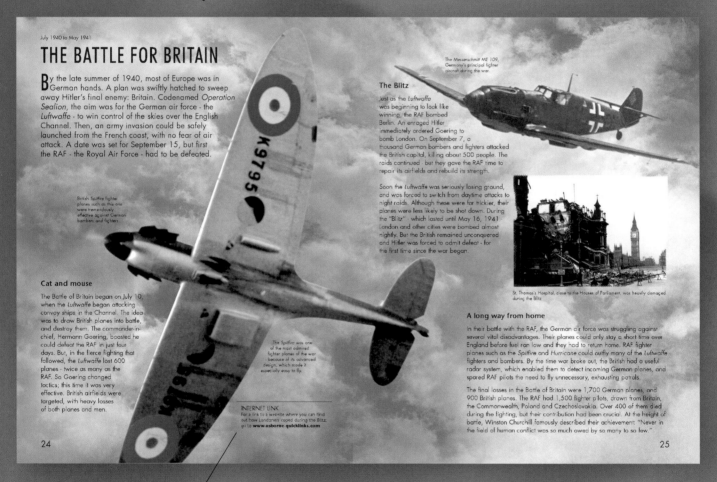

July 1940 to May 1941

THE BATTLE FOR BRITAIN

By the late summer of 1940, most of Europe was in German hands. A plan was swiftly hatched to sweep away Hitler's final enemy: Britain. Codenamed *Operation Sealion*, the aim was for the German air force - the *Luftwaffe* - to win control of the skies over the English Channel. Then, an army invasion could be safely launched from the French coast, with no fear of air attack. A date was set for September 15, but first the RAF - the Royal Air Force - had to be defeated.

British Spitfire fighter planes such as this one were tremendously effective against German bombers and fighters.

Cat and mouse

The Battle of Britain began on July 10, when the *Luftwaffe* began attacking convoy ships in the Channel. The idea was to draw British planes into battle, and destroy them. The commander-in-chief, Hermann Goering, boasted he could defeat the RAF in just four days. But, in the fierce fighting that followed, the *Luftwaffe* lost 600 planes - twice as many as the RAF. So Goering changed tactics; this time it was very effective. British airfields were targeted, with heavy losses of both planes and men.

The Spitfire was one of the most admired fighter planes of the war - because of its advanced design, which made it especially easy to fly.

INTERNET LINK
For a link to a website where you can find out how Londoners coped during the Blitz, go to **www.usborne-quicklinks.com**

24

The Messerschmitt ME 109, Germany's principal fighter aircraft during the war.

The Blitz

Just as the *Luftwaffe* was beginning to look like winning, the RAF bombed Berlin. An enraged Hitler immediately ordered Goering to bomb London. On September 7, a thousand German bombers and fighters attacked the British capital, killing about 500 people. The raids continued - but they gave the RAF time to repair its airfields and rebuild its strength.

Soon the *Luftwaffe* was seriously losing ground, and was forced to switch from daytime attacks to night raids. Although these were far trickier, their planes were less likely to be shot down. During the "Blitz" - which lasted until May 16, 1941 - London and other cities were bombed almost nightly. But the British remained unconquered and Hitler was forced to admit defeat - for the first time since the war began.

St. Thomas's Hospital, close to the Houses of Parliament, was heavily damaged during the Blitz.

A long way from home

In their battle with the RAF, the German air force was struggling against several vital disadvantages. Their planes could only stay a short time over England before fuel ran low and they had to return home. RAF fighter planes such as the *Spitfire* and *Hurricane* could outfly many of the *Luftwaffe* fighters and bombers. By the time war broke out, the British had a useful radar system, which enabled them to detect incoming German planes, and spared RAF pilots the need to fly unnecessary, exhausting patrols.

The final losses in the Battle of Britain were 1,700 German planes, and 900 British planes. The RAF had 1,500 fighter pilots, drawn from Britain, the Commonwealth, Poland and Czechoslovakia. Over 400 of them died during the fighting, but their contribution had been crucial. At the height of battle, Winston Churchill famously described their achievement: "Never in the field of human conflict was so much owed by so many to so few."

25

INTERNET LINK

For a link to a website where you can find out how Londoners coped during the Blitz, go to **www.usborne-quicklinks.com**

The links in Usborne Quicklinks are regularly updated, but occasionally you may find a site is unavailable. This may only be temporary so try again later, or even the next day.

1. Look for the "Internet link" boxes on the pages of this book. They contain descriptions of the websites you can visit.

2. In your computer's web browser, type the address **www.usborne-quicklinks.com** to go to the Usborne Quicklinks Website.

3. At the Usborne Quicklinks Website, type the keywords for the book: "world war two".

4. Type the page number of the link you want to visit. When the link appears, click on it to go to the recommended site.

Websites to visit

Here are some examples of the many things you can do on the websites recommended in this book:

• Go back in time to experience the day that war was declared

• Discover the fascinating real-life stories of bravery and heroism displayed by ordinary people

• Hear archive radio bulletins, reporting on the progress of the war

• Try your hand at leading a convoy of warships across the Atlantic Ocean

• Listen to eyewitness accounts of the Holocaust

• Watch bombers in flight and take a virtual tour of a *B-29 Superfortress*

Websites to visit

For information and help using the Internet, go to the Net Help area on the Usborne Quicklinks Website. You'll find information about "plug-ins" – small free programs that your web browser needs to play videos, animations and sounds. You probably already have these, but if not, you can download them for free from Quicklinks Net Help. You can also find information about computer viruses and advice on anti-virus software to protect your computer.

Staying safe online

Make sure you follow these simple rules to keep you safe online:

Children should ask an adult's permission before connecting to the Internet.

Never give out personal information about yourself, such as your real name, address, phone number or school.

If a site asks you to log in or register by typing in your name and address, children should ask permission from an adult first.

If you receive email from someone you don't know, don't reply to it. Tell an adult.

Adults – the websites described in this book are regularly reviewed and updated, but websites can change and Usborne Publishing is not responsible for any site other than its own. We recommend that children are supervised while on the Internet, that they do not use Internet chat rooms and that filtering software is used to block unsuitable material. You can find more information on Internet safety at the Usborne Quicklinks Website.

THE WORLD AT WAR

The Second World War was the most catastrophic conflict in history. Every continent on Earth was drawn into its fiery cauldron. Fought between two opposing alliances, known as the Allies and the Axis, the war began on September 1, 1939, when Germany invaded Poland. It ended six years and a day later with the official surrender of Germany's ally Japan on September 2, 1945. In that time, as many as 50 million men and women may have been killed.

Hitler in full cry, during a Nazi Party rally on the eve of the war

Allied powers

Under Axis control

Neutral countries

By the autumn of 1942, Germany and her Axis allies controlled all the territory shown here in red. Also marked are the captial cities of the major Allied and Axis powers, and the sites and dates of major battles.

FINLAND

SOVIET UNION

NORWAY

SWEDEN

Leningrad 1941-44

Moscow 1941

DENMARK

Kursk 1943

IRELAND

Battle of Britain 1940

Stalingrad 1942-43

BRITAIN

London

NETHERLANDS

POLAND

Berlin 1945

Warsaw Uprising 1944

BELGIUM

Normandy Landings 1944

Battle of the Bulge 1944

Paris

GREATER GERMANY

SLOVAKIA

RUMANIA

FRANCE

HUNGARY

SWITZERLAND

ITALY

YUGOSLAVIA

BULGARIA

TURKEY

SPAIN

Rome

GREECE

Territory under Allied control

El Alamein 1942

SAUDI ARABIA

EGYPT

These German soldiers are marching in a victory parade following the conquest of Poland in 1939. The distinctive march is called the goose step, and was kept for special ceremonial occasions.

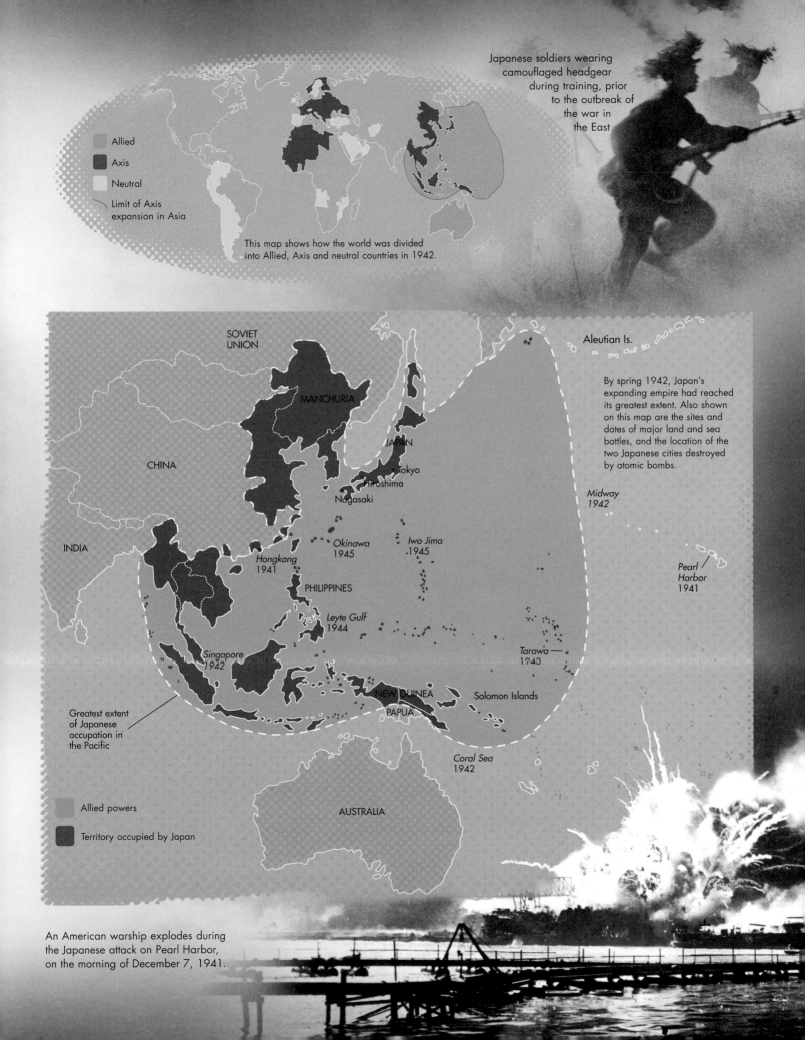

Allied
Axis
Neutral
Limit of Axis
expansion in Asia

This map shows how the world was divided
into Allied, Axis and neutral countries in 1942.

Japanese soldiers wearing
camouflaged headgear
during training, prior
to the outbreak of
the war in
the East

SOVIET
UNION

Aleutian Is.

MANCHURIA

By spring 1942, Japan's
expanding empire had reached
its greatest extent. Also shown
on this map are the sites and
dates of major land and sea
battles, and the location of the
two Japanese cities destroyed
by atomic bombs.

JAPAN

CHINA

Tokyo
Hiroshima
Nagasaki

Midway
1942

INDIA

Okinawa
1945

Iwo Jima
1945

Hongkong
1941

Pearl
Harbor
1941

PHILIPPINES

Leyte Gulf
1944

Singapore
1942

Tarawa
1940

NEW GUINEA

Solomon Islands

PAPUA

Greatest extent
of Japanese
occupation in
the Pacific

Coral Sea
1942

AUSTRALIA

Allied powers

Territory occupied by Japan

An American warship explodes during
the Japanese attack on Pearl Harbor,
on the morning of December 7, 1941.

THE RISE OF THE DICTATORS

The years after the First World War saw the rise of a new kind of political leader - the 20th century dictator. History is full of tyrants and monsters, but their powers were limited by the technology of their times. These new dictators used radio communication and broadcasts, to control every aspect of people's lives. Their whims and fancies destroyed millions of lives.

Mussolini, in full flow, addresses his fellow Italians in a New Year's Day speech in 1935.

A troubled world

The First World War left over 20 million dead, and dramatically redrew the map of Europe. Great empires and dynasties had fallen, and in the sullen peace that followed the victors nursed their wounds and the defeated yearned for revenge. Only America had done well out of the war, emerging as the world's most powerful nation.

Italian pioneer

The first great dictator to emerge from the ashes of war was a former teacher and journalist named Benito Mussolini - known to his people as *Il Duce* (meaning "the leader"). Italy had not benefitted from the war - although it had been on the winning side - and in the early 1920s, the country was crippled by strikes, street fighting between extremist political groups and general disorder. Mussolini, leader of the right-wing Fascist party, swept to power in 1922, promising to bring order and pride back to Italy. With tight control over the media and violent suppression of all opposition, he gave Italians the illusion that their country had become a thriving success. But his economic policies failed badly and he began to look abroad for a solution. Italy, he declared, should have a new Roman empire.

Hitler, on the eve of his seizure of power, uses his hypnotic gaze to full effect.

Hitler enters the stage

Germany had lost the war and her economy was in ruins. The worldwide Great Depression brought further misery to a country already suffering from massive unemployment after a decade of raging inflation.

Adolf Hitler, a former soldier and failed artist, offered the German people a clear solution to their problems. If they voted for him and his racist and ultra-right-wing Nazi Party, they would make the country great again and destroy the causes of Germany's misfortune. These Hitler named as Jews and communists. He came to power in 1933 and immediately began a process that would plunge the world into war and bring total ruin to his country.

INTERNET LINK
For a link to a website where you can explore the lives of Hitler, Stalin and Mussolini, go to
www.usborne-quicklinks.com

Japan's military leaders

Japan had been on the winning side in the First World War, but it too was suffering from serious economic problems as a result of the Great Depression. The military became increasingly involved in Japanese politics. They believed the solution to Japan's problems was to expand her empire - not only close to home in China, but over the whole of the Pacific, especially in territory controlled by fading colonial powers such as Britain, France and Holland.

Japan produced no individual dictator like Hitler or Mussolini, but the power of the military created an atmosphere just as oppressive as any dictatorship. "If there are any opposed to the 'Imperial Way' (Japanese expansion)," declared war minister General Ariki in 1933, "we shall give them an injection with a bullet and bayonet."

Foreign Minister Yosuke Matsuoka was one of many pre-war Japanese politicians who believed Japan should expand its empire.

The red czar

In Russia, the First World War had led directly to a communist revolution, and the country had been renamed the Soviet Union. When Lenin, the leader of the revolution, died in 1924, he was replaced by a wily Georgian named Joseph Stalin.

This photograph of Joseph Stalin shows some of the steely determination which allowed him to dominate the Soviet Union for three decades.

Stalin introduced vast changes in the Soviet Union, pushing through reforms that transformed the backward country into a powerful industrial nation. But he also had millions of people imprisoned and executed, including many officers of the Russian army - which became known as the Red Army.

The Russian communist rulers had much in common with the Nazis and Fascists - in their regulation of newspapers, radio and cinema; their suppression of all opposition; and their total control over people's lives.

THE FRAGILE DEMOCRACIES

An anxious crowd mills around Wall Street, on the day of the Wall Street Crash.

Such was the dreadful cost of the First World War that even most of its victors seemed like losers. France and Britain had begun the 20th century as the world's greatest powers. But in defending themselves against Germany to maintain that position, they had paid a terrible price. The United States, who had prospered in the war, retreated from the world stage. As the dictators waxed in power, the democracies waned before their eyes.

The empires strike back

In the 19th century, Britain, France and other European nations had built up large empires in Africa and Asia, which they controlled and exploited. The colonies were both markets for the goods of the occupying country, and suppliers of cheap raw materials. But, by the 1930s, many of them were costing more to rule than they were making. And many of the local people had begun protesting against occupation, and demanding independence.

All fall down

In 1929, the US stock market failed. This event, which became known as the *Wall Street Crash*, triggered a serious economic slump, resulting in widespread unemployment, poverty and starvation. Imports to US factories and shops were seriously reduced, and overseas loans from American banks were recalled. The *Great Depression*, as it was known, affected countries throughout the world, from Britain to Japan.

Unwanted responsibilities

After the First World War, the United States emerged as the wealthiest and most powerful nation on Earth. American banks lent vast sums of money to the war-ravaged countries of Europe, while countries all over the world exported materials and goods to American factories and shops.

But many American citizens did not want their country to be involved in foreign entanglements - especially in another overseas war. This policy, called Isolationism, would later turn out to be unrealistic for America - and would have been disastrous for the rest of the world.

Fear of war

Because the First World War had caused such carnage, the victorious countries were determined to prevent another war from happening, especially as the new generation of bomber aircraft and poison gas would be able to cause terrible destruction to cities. During the 1930s, many people actively campaigned for peace. Politicians such as Winston Churchill, who talked of standing up to the dictators and preparing for war, were unpopular.

The League of Nations

After the First World War, an international organization called the League of Nations was set up in Geneva. It was a forerunner of the United Nations. The countries that joined pledged to settle their disputes without resorting to war. Member nations could show their disapproval of other countries by enforcing economic sanctions. But the League had two major flaws: the United States never joined, and there was no armed force to back up its decisions. Japan, Germany and Italy were all members, but they all left when their aggressive foreign policies were condemned by the League.

The Maginot Line

In case of war, the French hoped to defend their border against Germany with the Maginot Line - a string of underground forts, 140km (87 mile) long, built during the 1930s at a cost of $200 million. It was a formidable obstacle, but when war came, Hitler's armies simply avoided it, sweeping into France through Luxembourg and Belgium.

INTERNET LINK
For a link to a website where you can see more photographs of the Great Depression, go to
www.usborne-quicklinks.com

Unemployed Americans in Brooklyn, New York, line up for free food, during the Great Depression.

HITLER'S GERMANY

When the Nazis came to power in 1933, the British ambassador to Berlin, Sir Horace Rumbold, commented, "Many of us... have a feeling that we are living in a country where fantastic hooligans and eccentrics have got the upper hand." Only the Soviet Union could rival their sinister lunacy. But there was method in their madness. Hitler put his country back to work, and by 1939 Germany had become the most powerful nation in Europe.

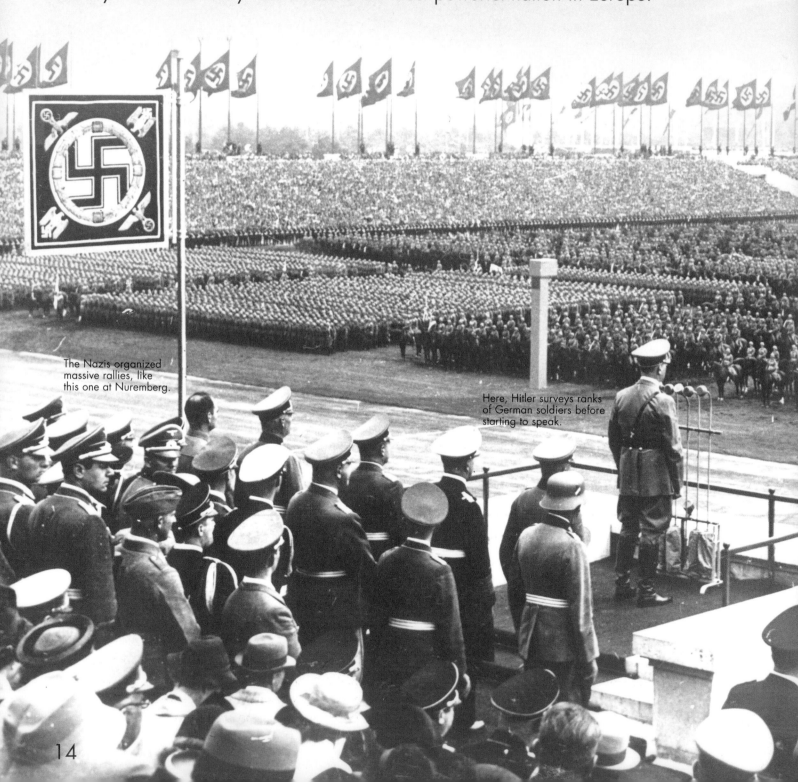

The Nazis organized massive rallies, like this one at Nuremberg.

Here, Hitler surveys ranks of German soldiers before starting to speak.

Nazi propaganda

Once in power, the Nazis set about transforming their country into a reflection of their own crooked image. Radio, cinema, newspapers and magazines pumped out an endless stream of Nazi propaganda. Rallies and torchlit parades were held to reinforce their message - which could be summed up by three main points, made plain in Hitler's political testament, *Mein Kampf*.

- The Jews were the enemy of mankind, and should be destroyed.
- Communism too, should be eradicated.
- The Aryan race (people of pure Germanic blood), led by Hitler, should conquer and enslave the Slavs of Eastern Europe and Russia.

Back to work

The Nazis solved Germany's unemployment problem with ambitious public construction projects - grand new government buildings and a motorway system were built. Women were forced out of jobs and replaced by men. New jobs were created in armaments factories and in the armed forces. By 1939 Germany was a prosperous and formidably-armed country.

INTERNET LINK
For a link to a website where you can take a photo tour of the Nuremberg rally grounds, go to
www.usborne-quicklinks.com

Race hate

At the very heart of Nazi policy was a deeply-felt hatred of Jews. As soon as the Nazis came to power, Jews were expelled from government and university jobs. Jewish shops were attacked, and Jews were bullied and humiliated in the streets. Many left. Others could not afford to go, or just hoped things would get better. But their future was bleak. Germans were also taught to despise other racial groups, such as the Slavs, Gypsies and Negroes. The Nazis called them *untermensch*, which meant "sub-human" in German.

A Hitler Youth drum and bugle corps plays a fanfare during the beginning of a Nazi ceremony. Hitler believed that German boys should be prepared for war from an early age.

Snaring the young

Along with their corrosive anti-Semitism, perhaps the most disturbing thing about the Nazis was the way they tried to corrupt the minds of German children. Nazi ideas, especially on race, were taught as part of the school curriculum. Young boys joined an organization called the Hitler Youth, where they learned how to be soldiers. Young girls joined the League of German Maidens where they were taught that their greatest role in life was to provide boys for Hitler's armies.

Here is a question from a school mathematics textbook, used during the Nazi era: *"A bomber on takeoff carries 12 dozen bombs each weighing 10 kilos. The aircraft makes for Warsaw, the heart of international Jewry. It bombs the town. On takeoff, with all bombs on board and a fuel tank containing 1500 kilos of fuel, the aircraft weighs 8 tonnes. When it returns from the crusade there are still 230 kilos of fuel left. What is the weight of the aircraft when empty?"*

THE ROAD TO WAR

The 1930s were a dark and difficult decade. As the world struggled to recover from the Depression, Japan, Italy and Germany seized territory from other nations. The League of Nations, founded to prevent further wars, made feeble protests. But the dictators grew bolder. Would *anything* they did provoke retaliation?

1931

Japan invades the Chinese region of Manchuria, hoping to expand her empire in Asia. The League of Nations protests, but without success.

October 1935-May 1936

Italy invades Ethiopia from her nearby colonies of Eritrea and Somaliland. Barefooted tribesmen lose an eight-month battle against Italian forces, who use poison gas and bombers against them. The League of Nations protests, and imposes sanctions. But these are ineffective and are soon lifted.

British Prime Minister Neville Chamberlain with Hitler, September 1938

March 1936

German troops march into the Rhineland - the border region between Germany and France. According to the terms of the Treaty of Versailles, at the end of the First World War, this was supposed to be free of military forces.

July 1936-1939

General Francisco Franco leads a rebellion against Spain's left-wing government. Italy and Germany send arms and men to help him. In 1939, Franco wins and Spain becomes a fascist state. The bombing of Spanish towns by German aircraft increases the desire for peace in France and Britain.

October-November 1936

Germany, Italy and Japan discuss the formation of an anti-communist alliance, known as the Rome-Berlin-Tokyo Axis - later known as the "Axis" powers.

1937-1938

Japanese forces seize the main ports of China. The Japanese army commits atrocities in the city of Nanjing - a deliberate warning to China not to resist.

March 1938

German troops enter Austria, and unite the country with Germany. Known as the *Anschluss*, this had also been forbidden by the Versailles Treaty.

August-September 1938

Hitler claims the Sudetenland, an area of Czechoslovakia where people speak German, should be part of Germany. The British and French prime ministers fly to Munich for crisis talks. Their countries are ill-prepared for war. There is also a feeling that Germany had been badly treated after the First World War and had grounds for complaint.

This results in a policy of "appeasement" - giving in to German demands. The British and French allow Germany to take over Sudetenland. Hitler declares, "I have no more territorial demands to make in Europe." But it is a blatant lie.

March 1939

German troops seize western Czechoslovakia, and occupy Prague. The British and French realize appeasement has failed. Hitler's next obvious target, Poland, is offered military help. Rapid rearmament and conscription begins.

Summer 1939

As Hitler prepares Germany for the invasion of Poland, Britain, France and the Soviet Union have half-hearted discussions about an alliance against Germany.

August 1939

In a move which astonishes the world, sworn enemies Nazi Germany and Soviet Russia announce they have signed a non-aggression pact - promising not to attack each other. A secret clause divides Poland between them.

In Germany, military commanders are worried Hitler is set to take a disastrous gamble and commit their country to a war it cannot win. Hitler reassures them that after the conquest of Poland, Britain and France will be anxious to make peace with Germany.

INTERNET LINK
For links to websites with slide shows, documents and film clips of events during the 1930s, go to
www.usborne-quicklinks.com

German troops march through the gates of Hradschin Castle, Prague, during the occupation of the Czech capital in 1938.

September 1939 to June 1941

WAR BEGINS IN EUROPE

Residents of Warsaw get their first look at the German invaders, as motorcycle troops trundle over tramlines in the Polish capital on October 1, 1939. The occupation would last over four years and almost all the city would be destroyed.

WAR BREAKS OUT

The Second World War began in the hours before the dawn of September 1, 1939, when Nazi troops and aircraft flooded over Germany's eastern border and into Poland. This prompted Poland's allies Britain and France to declare war on Germany on September 3. Within two years the war would turn from a European to a global conflict, which lasted until September 2, 1945.

INTERNET LINK
For a link to a website where you can watch archive footage of Germany's invasion of Poland, go to **www.usborne-quicklinks.com**

German SS troops seek shelter behind a tank, during the invasion of the Baltic port of Danzig. If you look carefully, you can see the SS "death's head" insignia on the tank.

A new way of fighting

The first week of September saw a succession of beautiful late summer days – perfect for the German army to try its new tactic of *Blitzkrieg* – meaning *lightning war*. First, squadrons of bombers flew deep into Poland, destroying air bases, fuel and ammunition dumps, railway stations and military headquarters. Then, dive bombers screamed down to machine-gun and bomb Polish front line troops. Tanks and troop-carrying vehicles probed the Polish lines for weak spots, bursting through to attack strong points from behind. Large numbers of foot soldiers followed, to mop up any remaining resistance. The idea of *Blitzkrieg* was not a new one, but the Germans were the first to try it.

Dirty tricks

The invasion of Poland started with a bizarre charade known as "Operation Canned Goods" – staged by Germany to justify the attack. SS soldiers executed 12 ordinary criminals dressed in Polish army uniforms, and placed the bodies around a German radio station near the Polish border. Then they announced that the Poles had attacked the radio station. Journalists and press photographers were called in to record the grisly hoax.

Polish army cavalry units like this one were sent to fight German tanks - but they were cut to pieces.

20

The fate of Poland

Poland lost control of the war in the first two or three days. Although the Poles had a larger army than the Germans, they had fewer tanks and aircraft. The Polish front line quickly crumbled. Thousands of fleeing civilians clogged the roads away from the fighting, preventing reinforcements from coming forward. The Polish cavalry was sent to attack German tanks - but with predictably disastrous results. The Polish capital Warsaw was heavily bombed, causing further panic and disruption. Within a week, the German army had reached the outskirts of Warsaw. The city finally surrendered on September 27.

Trouble from the East

On September 17, when most of the fighting was over, Poland was also invaded by Soviet troops. They swiftly occupied land that had secretly been given to the Soviet Union during negotiations for the Nazi-Soviet Pact.

"Close your hearts to pity"

The Nazis saw the Poles as subhuman - fit only for slavery. On the eve of the attack, Hitler told his generals: "Close your hearts to pity. Act brutally. Whatever we find in the shape of an upper class in Poland is to be liquidated…" Close behind came squads of SS *Einsatzgruppen* (special forces), with orders to find and kill Jews, and anyone - priests, teachers, aristocrats - who might organize resistance. "House cleaning" was how the Nazis described this.

The worms turn

Hitler knew his attack on Poland carried the risk of war with France and Britain, but he was full of contempt for them. "They are little worms," he said. "I saw them at Munich. I'll cook them a stew they'll choke on." But the worms turned. Britain and France declared war on September 3. Germany now had two powerful enemies on its western border.

THE FALL OF WESTERN EUROPE

After his whirlwind success in Poland, Hitler hoped the French and British would be eager to make peace. But he was to be disappointed. During the winter months, fighting almost came to a standstill. The Germans called this phase of the war *Sitzkreig*; the British called it the *Bore War*. It was the calm before the storm. When winter passed, the war began in earnest. Once again, *Blitzkrieg* proved very successful for the Germans.

German troops, heading for the English Channel, storm through a village in the first days of their invasion of France.

Slow start

At the start of the war, there was a sudden change of pace in France and Britain. People began to carry gas masks wherever they went, in case the German air force dropped gas bombs. Children were evacuated from cities, and sent to live in the country. But after a few weeks, when nothing happened, there was a sense of anticlimax. Fighting began again in the Spring of 1940, and brought a series of brilliant German victories.

The war heats up

On April 9, Nazi troops invaded Norway and Denmark. The Norwegians resisted the invaders until June 9. The Danes surrendered within hours. These further Nazi triumphs forced British Prime Minister Neville Chamberlain to resign. He was replaced by Winston Churchill, a famously staunch opponent of Hitler's. On May 10, German armies invaded Western Europe, and troops poured into Belgium and Holland. Within four days, Holland surrendered. Belgium was overrun by May 28. On May 13 the Germans unleashed a massive *Blitzkrieg* offensive in the French Ardennes region on France's Belgian border. Fresh from their recent triumphs in Poland, German tanks and soldiers, under General Heinz Guderian, reached the English Channel in a week.

INTERNET LINK

For a link to a website where you can watch a movie that gives you a glimpse of what it was like to be at the Dunkirk evacuation, go to **www.usborne-quicklinks.com**

A small miracle

Guderian's forces cut the Allied armies in two. Those stranded to the north were caught in a narrow pocket around the French port of Dunkirk. In an extraordinary few days, a fleet of 900 British ferries, sailing boats and navy vessels, helped by the French navy, rescued over 200,000 British troops and around 110,000 French, Dutch and Belgian troops.

The map of Europe in summer 1940

- 🔴 Axis powers
- 🔴 Areas under Axis control
- ⚪ Allied nations
- 🔴 Neutral nations

In less than a year, German armies conquered Poland, Norway, Denmark, Holland, Belgium and France. But Britain remained undefeated.

These British troops on the beach at Dunkirk, are surrounded by abandoned equipment and dead and wounded comrades. They had only their rifles to defend themselves from constant air attack by German dive bombers.

On to Paris

As the British withdrew from the continent, the German army pressed on to Paris. The French capital fell on June 14, a month after the invasion. A week later, France surrendered. Hitler was ecstatic. In the First World War, a million Germans had died in four years, trying to defeat France. Now Germany had succeeded in less than six weeks, at a cost of a mere 27,000 lives.

National humiliation

With characteristic spitefulness, Hitler ordered the French surrender to be signed in the same railway carriage that the French had used to accept the German surrender in the First World War. France was now divided into two. The north and west was occupied by the Germans. The south was ruled by the Vichy government - French politicians who collaborated with the Germans. The victory over France was Hitler's greatest military triumph. But although the future held further success, the tide would slowly turn against him.

Here, a week after the surrender, Hitler makes a dawn tour of Paris.

THE BATTLE FOR BRITAIN

By the late summer of 1940, most of Europe was in German hands. A plan was swiftly hatched to sweep away Hitler's final enemy: Britain. Codenamed *Operation Sealion*, the aim was for the German air force - the *Luftwaffe* - to win control of the skies over the English Channel. Then, an army invasion could be safely launched from the French coast, with no fear of air attack. A date was set for September 15, but first the RAF - the Royal Air Force - had to be defeated.

British *Spitfire* fighter planes such as this one were tremendously effective against German bombers and fighters.

Cat and mouse

The Battle of Britain began on July 10, when the *Luftwaffe* began attacking convoy ships in the Channel. The idea was to draw British planes into battle, and destroy them. The commander-in-chief, Hermann Goering, boasted he could defeat the RAF in just four days. But, in the fierce fighting that followed, the *Luftwaffe* lost 600 planes - twice as many as the RAF. So Goering changed tactics; this time it was very effective. British airfields were targeted, with heavy losses of both planes and men.

The *Spitfire* was one of the most admired fighter planes of the war - because of its advanced design, which made it especially easy to fly.

INTERNET LINK
For a link to a website where you can find out how Londoners coped during the Blitz, go to **www.usborne-quicklinks.com**

The *Messerschmitt ME 109*, Germany's principal fighter aircraft during the war.

The Blitz

Just as the *Luftwaffe* was beginning to look like winning, the RAF bombed Berlin. An enraged Hitler immediately ordered Goering to bomb London. On September 7, a thousand German bombers and fighters attacked the British capital, killing about 500 people. The raids continued - but they gave the RAF time to repair its airfields and rebuild its strength.

Soon the *Luftwaffe* was seriously losing ground, and was forced to switch from daytime attacks to night raids. Although these were far trickier, their planes were less likely to be shot down. During the "Blitz" - which lasted until May 16, 1941 - London and other cities were bombed almost nightly. But the British remained unconquered and Hitler was forced to admit defeat - for the first time since the war began.

St. Thomas's Hospital, close to the Houses of Parliament, was heavily damaged during the Blitz.

A long way from home

In their battle with the RAF, the German air force was struggling against several vital disadvantages. Their planes could only stay a short time over England before fuel ran low and they had to return home. RAF fighter planes such as the *Spitfire* and *Hurricane* could outfly many of the *Luftwaffe* fighters and bombers. By the time war broke out, the British had a useful radar system, which enabled them to detect incoming German planes, and spared RAF pilots the need to fly unnecessary, exhausting patrols.

The final losses in the Battle of Britain were 1,700 German planes, and 900 British planes. The RAF had 1,500 fighter pilots, drawn from Britain, the Commonwealth, Poland and Czechoslovakia. Over 400 of them died during the fighting, but their contribution had been crucial. At the height of battle, Winston Churchill famously described their achievement: "Never in the field of human conflict was so much owed by so many to so few."

GERMANY INVADES EASTERN EUROPE

With his enemies in Western Europe defeated, and Britain bloodied, Hitler began to plan the invasion of Russia. But, before he could, a series of crises in Eastern Europe demanded his attention. The most vexing of these was caused by Germany's own ally, Italy.

Italy joins the war

Although they were Axis allies, Mussolini did not commit his country to Hitler's war in Europe until he was sure the Germans would win. In the final stages of Hitler's campaign in Western Europe, Italy invaded France from the south.

With France defeated, Italian troops invaded the small colony of British Somaliland, which they managed to take in August 1940. This was their one success of the entire war - although it was seized back by the British within a year. In September they launched an invasion of British-occupied Egypt, from their colony of Libya, only to have their tanks run out of fuel 100km (60 miles) over the border. The British responded with retaliatory attacks on Libya. A disastrous invasion of Greece followed in October. The Italians were expelled within weeks, and lost half their battleships at Taranto.

German troops prepare to board transport planes to take them to Crete, in June 1941.

A powerful friend

Mussolini had desperately wanted to show the world that his Fascist Italy could be just as successful as Nazi Germany. He talked boastfully of "a new Roman empire" and referred to the Mediterranean Sea as "an Italian lake". Now, Hitler had to rescue his ally. German troops, rested and confident after their recent victories, flooded into Libya to save it from the British. The following spring, Greece was invaded again, together with Yugoslavia. Yugoslavia fell in little more than a week, but it would prove to be far easier to overrun than to hold on to. Hundreds of thousands of Yugoslavian soldiers disappeared into the mountains and forests, to harass the occupying German army for the rest of the war.

Mediterranean victories

The Germans took the Greek mainland within a month. Then, in a final military masterstroke, they invaded Crete. Hitler was determined that his one supply of oil, the Ploesti oilfields in Rumania, should be safe from British airbases in Greece and Crete.

In the first fully airborne invasion in history, 20,000 German soldiers parachuted onto the island or landed by glider. Facing them were over 40,000 Allied troops - from Britain, Greece, Crete, Australia and New Zealand. Although over 7,000 Germans were killed, their opponents were poorly equipped and worn out from fighting in Greece. The Germans captured the island within 10 days; it was to be one of Hitler's last great victories.

INTERNET LINK
For a link to a website where you can watch a slide show of Germany's invasion of Greece, go to
www.usborne-quicklinks.com

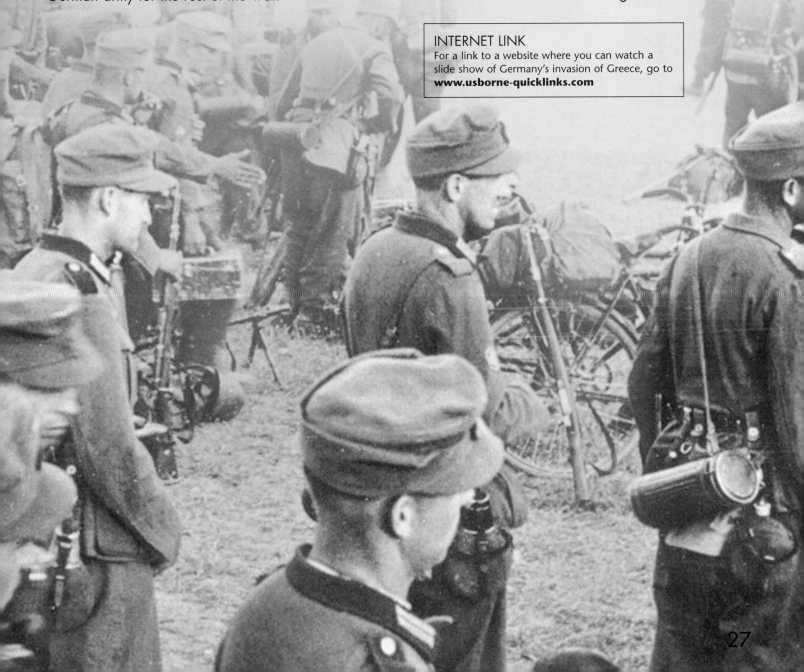

27

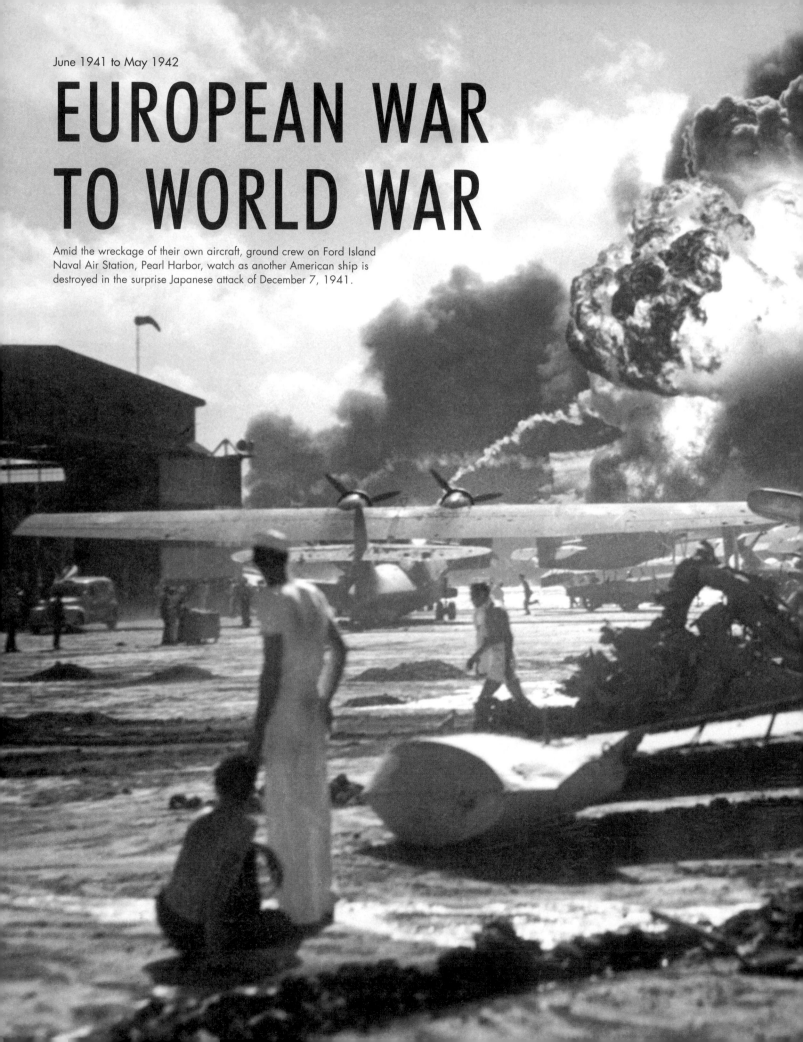

June 1941 to May 1942

EUROPEAN WAR TO WORLD WAR

Amid the wreckage of their own aircraft, ground crew on Ford Island Naval Air Station, Pearl Harbor, watch as another American ship is destroyed in the surprise Japanese attack of December 7, 1941.

OPERATION BARBAROSSA

On the dawn of June 22, 1941, the greatest invasion in the history of the world began. It was codenamed *Operation Barbarossa*. Three million German troops, and thousands of tanks and planes, poured over the Soviet border. They intended to conquer the world's largest country by the end of the summer. And they nearly did.

The arrows on this map show the routes of German troops into the Soviet Union during *Operation Barbarossa*.

Confidence man

Hitler was so confident of success, he bragged to his generals: "We have only to kick in the door, and the whole rotten structure will come crashing down." On that June day three German army groups - North, Central and South - struck out for Leningrad (now St. Petersburg), Moscow and the Ukraine.

The German armies moved forward rapidly - employing the *Blitzkrieg* tactics that had won them easy victories in Poland and France. Soviet troops were totally disorganized. Stalin himself was so stunned by the attack, he spent 11 days in almost complete isolation, barely believing his former ally had betrayed him so ruthlessly.

Mistaken welcome

In some parts of the Soviet Union, especially Latvia, Estonia, Lithuania and the Ukraine, the Germans were welcomed as liberators. Many people there hated the tyrannous communist rule of Joseph Stalin. But this warm welcome soon changed to hostility and resistance. The Nazis regarded the people of the Soviet Union as slaves, and behaved towards them with great arrogance and brutality.

INTERNET LINK
For a link to a website where you can read eyewitness accounts of *Operation Barbarossa*, go to
www.usborne-quicklinks.com

Leningrad and Moscow besieged

The war was not won by the end of the summer, but Leningrad was beseiged and, by early October, German soldiers had reached the suburbs of Moscow. They were so close, they could see the Kremlin's famous golden domes. But the first snow of winter had fallen, and autumn rain had turned roads to slush. Hitler had been so confident of a speedy victory, his soldiers had not been supplied with warm clothing, or winter equipment. Supplies were running out too, and men were weary from four months' fighting.

Some Soviet citizens, like these Ukrainian women, initially greeted the Nazis as "liberators" - but they quickly changed their minds.

This German soldier strides past an exploding amunition dump, during the German invasion of Soviet Russia.

Ominous signs

But there was something else too, even more significant. "In spite of the distances we were advancing," wrote one German soldier, "there was no feeling, as there had been in France, of entry into a defeated nation. Instead there was resistance, always resistance, however hopeless." At this early stage of the war, the Russians had lost a phenomenal two and a half million men, as well as over 20,000 artillery guns, 18,000 tanks and 14,000 aircraft - but still they fought on. Hitler received reports of mounting Soviet resistance. "The Russians fight with a truly stupid fanaticism," he fretted.

These Soviet women, photographed in summer 1941, have joined a guerilla force to fight the Nazis in occupied territory.

A great cause

In an ironic twist of fate, the Nazi's cruelty united the Russian people in a way their communist leaders never could. To millions of Russians, the struggle against the Germans became "the Great Patriotic War" - and they fought with magnificent bravery to rid their homeland of these savage invaders.

On December 6, 1941, in temperatures of -60°C, fresh Soviet troops launched an attack on the German army in the outskirts of Moscow. The exhausted Germans withdrew a little, to strong defensive positions. There they readied themselves for a further assault in the spring.

THE SIEGE OF LENINGRAD

During the summer of 1941, the German army advanced deep into Soviet Russia. By mid-July Army Group North had made 800km (500 miles) in three weeks. Its target was Leningrad, the beautiful, historic city now called St. Petersburg. Hitler declared that the city would, "fall like a leaf." By early September, Leningrad's three million inhabitants were surrounded, and occupation seemed only days away.

A Red Army machine-gunner defends the outskirts of Leningrad during the three-year siege.

Changing plans

As the Germans approached, Leningrad prepared to fight to the end. Over 160km (100 miles) of anti-tank ditches were built, and buildings were booby-trapped. But, just as the Nazis reached the gates of the city, there was a sudden change of plan. Many of the troops were sent south, to take part in an assault on Moscow. So instead of a full-scale attack on Leningrad, it was decided to starve and bombard the city into submission.

Half rations, and less

Its population swollen by refugees fleeing the Nazi advance, Leningrad needed huge amounts of food each day. But the only routes left into the city were a small airstrip and a ferry via Lake Ladoga to the east. As winter arrived, the amount of food getting in was barely half what was needed - and worse was to come. By November, the besieged citizens were living on starvation rations.

Fear stalks the city

In desperation, people ate horses, cats, dogs, rodents - even grass. The only water supply was from the Neva, which ran through the city. Some even turned to cannibalism. It was said that people were afraid to leave their homes, in case they were killed and eaten. In the midst of all this suffering, there was also constant artillery and aerial bombardment. The streets were littered with dead bodies, killed by the bombs or from starvation. By winter, it wasn't possible to bury them, as the ground had frozen solid.

Citizens scurry between the dead and exploding artillery shells, in Leningrad's main street, Nevsky Prospekt.

Winter relief

But the winter freeze brought good news too. Lake Ladoga froze so solid, it was possible to drive heavy supply trucks over it. By January 1942, 400 trucks a day were coming into the city, taking out refugees on their return journey. The trucks often came under heavy fire, or crashed into craters and holes in the ice, but they saved the city from starvation.

In spring, the thaw cut off the truck supply route across the lake, although food continued to come in by boat. But the warmer weather bought further misery. As frozen corpses thawed and began to rot, an epidemic swept through the city, killing thousands.

INTERNET LINK

For a link to a website where you can find out more about what life was like in Leningrad during the seige, go to **www.usborne-quicklinks.com**

The end in sight

But the worst was over. As the ground softened, the bodies were swiftly buried, and a pipeline laid under the lake began to deliver fuel. Leningrad could sense it was winning, and celebrated with a concert in its Philharmonic Hall, performed by musicians recalled from the front. The music - the 7th (or Leningrad) Symphony - was written especially by Dmitri Shostakovich, one of its most famous citizens. The concert was broadcast and German soldiers who listened in became demoralized. Leningrad did not sound at all like a city on the brink of defeat.

December 7 1941

PEARL HARBOR

One sleepy Sunday morning, on December 7, 1941, Japanese planes made a dramatic attack on the American naval base at Pearl Harbor, Hawaii. This one act changed the course of the war irretrievably. America declared war on Japan, and Japan's allies, Germany and Italy, declared war on America. The Axis powers would soon discover just what a formidable and determined opponent she would be.

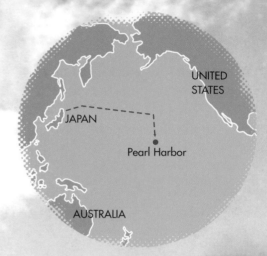

The Japanese launched their surprise attack on Pearl Harbor (route shown in red) from halfway across the Pacific Ocean.

A daring move

Pearl Harbor is a massive naval base in a natural inlet on Oahu Island, Hawaii. It was, and still is, the headquarters of the US Pacific Fleet. Also on the island are seven airfields, dry docks to repair ships, a submarine base and huge oil storage facilities. Japan was not at war with America at the time of the attack. But she hoped to land such a stunning blow on her Pacific rival that she would be able to seize vast swathes of territory before the United States recovered.

INTERNET LINK
For a link to a website where you can watch film footage and listen to radio broadcasts reporting the attack on Pearl Harbor, go to **www.usborne-quicklinks.com**

Disturbing the peace

The attack was timed to take place when American forces would be at their least alert. It worked like a dream: around 90% of all damage occurred in the first 10 minutes. A fleet of six aircraft carriers and 26 support ships had sailed from Japan 11 days earlier. Undetected, they arrived at their launch zone the night before, 450km (700 miles) north of Hawaii. Midget submarines, which had sneaked into the inlet, joined the attack. After half an hour of carnage and chaos, Japanese planes vanished from the sky.

Three American battleships burn in Pearl Harbor, in the aftermath of the attack. Pictured here are *West Virginia*, *Tennessee* and *Arizona*.

34

Strike two

As American service personnel battled with fires and tended to the wounded, another 170 Japanese planes arrived for a second strike. For an hour they wheeled around the base, but this second attack was less successful. The Americans were now operating their anti-aircraft guns, and Japanese pilots faced determined opposition.

Easy targets

As a result of the Japanese attacks, 18 warships were sunk or damaged, 180 aircraft were destroyed, and 2,400 Americans were killed. They had all made easy targets: the ships in the inlet had been grouped in pairs and the planes in the airbases had been bunched together. The worst casualties occurred aboard the battleship *Arizona*. During the first attack, a bomb dropped right down her funnel, and set off an explosion which killed a thousand men in a single blinding flash.

Waking the sleeping tiger

The United States was outraged by the attack and declared war immediately. A stunned population heard their president, Franklin D. Roosevelt, describe December 7 as, "a date that will live in infamy." Overnight, the war was transformed from a European conflict into a global one. It was especially good news for Britain and Russia, who had been struggling to survive against Nazi Germany. Now they had America, the most powerful nation on earth, to fight beside them. Even the man who had been ordered to plan the Pearl Harbor raid, Admiral Isoruku Yamamoto, had grave misgivings. "I fear we have only succeeded in awakening a sleeping tiger," he told fellow officers.

Admiral Isoruku Yamamoto, Commander-in-Chief of the Japanese Combined Fleet, consults sea charts as he plans an attack.

35

JAPAN'S NEW EMPIRE

Following the devastating attack at Pearl Harbor, Japan's military leaders knew they had to act fast to create their new Japanese empire before America recovered its strength. In the lightning campaign that followed, the Japanese conquered most of the Asian Pacific seaboard, and looked set to invade India and Australia.

Japan's new empire (shown here in dark pink) took in mainland Asia and great swathes of the Pacific.

Runaway success

Before the attack, Admiral Yamamoto had promised, "a wild show for six months. But," he went on to say, "if the war drags on two or three years I cannot be confident of the outcome." His words were prophetic. The first six months saw Japanese successes that overshadowed even Hitler's victories. Their targets were the Allies' colonies in the Pacific and the Far East. Before the year ended, they had captured Hong Kong and invaded Burma, Malaya, Borneo and the Philippines. In February 1942, they defeated British troops in Singapore that outnumbered them almost three to one.

A friendly face?

Japanese propaganda described this sudden expansion of her empire as the "Greater East Asian Co-Prosperity Sphere" and coined a slogan "Asia for the Asiatics". But, within days of occupation, the conquered peoples quickly came to realize that the Japanese were no better - and frequently worse - than the European powers that had previously ruled over them. In a deliberate policy to encourage citizens to surrender rather than fight, they were subjected to indiscriminate massacres and rape by the Japanese army.

Why Japan succeeded

Japan achieved these extraordinary victories by having several clear advantages over its enemies. At the beginning, the Japanese navy controlled the sea, and could protect the troop ships needed to ferry soldiers to these new territories. The forces defending many of the places they attacked were weak, and the Japanese army fought with greater ferocity, often defeating opponents who outnumbered them.

Show's over?

By May 1942, Japanese fighting forces had more than exceeded expectations. The plan now was to defend the newly conquered territories so fiercely that America and Britain would have to accept that they had lost them. But the Japanese had underestimated the United States, and the stunned outrage they had provoked. After inspecting the damage at Pearl Harbor, one American admiral vowed, "Before we're through with them, the Japanese language will be spoken only in hell." In spring 1942, America was about to strike back, and Japan's moment of triumph had passed.

A Japanese soldier stands guard over American prisoners in the Philippines, on New Year's Day, 1942.

37

UNDERGROUND RESISTANCE

The Germans and Japanese behaved with great brutality towards the nations they occupied and exploited. In the Pacific, conquered people were usually too shocked and frightened to offer further resistance. But in Europe and Russia - and to a lesser extent in Malaya, Burma and the Philippines - the occupying forces found that the citizens of the nations they so arrogantly ruled were prepared to fight back.

Resistance in the West

In Western Europe resistance was often low-key. People would walk out of cafés when German soldiers came in, or make other small gestures to make them feel unwelcome. But the French had groups of underground fighters, known as the French Resistance. Some lived ordinary lives in towns and villages, venturing out at night in secret to blow up German trains, or carry out hit-and-run raids on military bases or convoys. Others fled to forests and hills to live as outlaws in armed groups. They were known as the *Maquis*, after a French word for a kind of bush.

Other means

Resistance didn't just mean fighting Germans. Some people helped by hiding downed pilots, escaped prisoners-of-war, or fleeing Jews, as they made their perilous journeys to England. Others printed illegal newspapers, or discreetly sabotaged factory machinery, or stole military maps from under the noses of their enemy.

INTERNET LINK

For a link to a website where you can read fascinating stories of resistance fighters, go to **www.usborne-quicklinks.com**

Eastern Europe

Resistance was even fiercer in Eastern Europe, partly because the Nazis behaved with even greater savagery there. After the invasion of the Soviet Union, 88 million people lived under Nazi control. Bands of underground fighters, known as partisans, fought a protracted guerrilla war against them. Blowing up supply trains and railway lines was especially effective. Thousands of German troops had to be diverted from the front, to try to keep the partisans under control.

Fierce retaliation

Wherever resistance attacks took place, the Nazis reacted with vicious reprisals against the local people. In 1942, leading Nazi Reinhard Heydrich was assassinated in Prague by exiled members of the Czech army. As well as hunting down his killers, and hundreds of other suspects, the Nazis destroyed the Czech village of Lidice, executed the men and sent the women and children to concentration and death camps. In all, 5,000 were murdered in retaliation for the assassination.

Success in Yugoslavia

Perhaps the most successful resistance group of all was a band of Yugoslav partisans lead by Josip Tito, which grew to many thousands strong. They fought a constant campaign against the Germans for much of the occupation, taking over most of the northwest of the country. In October 1944, Tito's forces liberated the Yugoslav capital, Belgrade, driving the Nazis out. Yugoslavia became the only conquered country to free itself from Nazi rule without substantial help from abroad.

This band of Soviet partisans sheltering around a fire was photographed in 1943. Some are civilians who have taken up arms; others are soldiers who have fallen behind enemy lines.

THE HOME FRONT

Such was the scale and ferocity of the war, that many countries devoted almost their entire populations and resources to winning it. Women were recruited into factories and other areas of work previously reserved for men. For the citizens of the major fighting nations, the war became an inescapable part of their everyday lives - even for those who were lucky enough to escape the horror of bombing.

Hard times

During the invasion of Russia, 1,500 factories were moved east, away from the rapid German advance. Six million Russians, mainly women, were uprooted and sent to work in them. They had no choice in what they did, and had to work wherever they were sent. They built tanks like the very effective *T-34*. Produced in their thousands, away from the threat of German bombing, these tanks were crucial in helping the Soviets win their war against Nazi Germany.

Close to the front line, Soviet citizens toil to produce weapons in an underground factory, where they are safe from Nazi artillery and aerial attack.

This British woman carefully drills components for an RAF *Spitfire*, at an aircraft production factory in Southampton, England, in early 1940.

Arsenal of democracy

President Roosevelt declared that America would become the "arsenal of democracy" - arming itself and its allies in the fight against tyranny. American women flocked to factories to replace men called up for military service. Shipbuilding increased by 600%, and aircraft production by 500%. By 1944, one new plane was being built every five minutes. American armaments factories, like Russia's, were outside the range of enemy bombers.

This rate of production gave the United States a formidable advantage over Germany and Japan. Britain and the Soviet Union both used large quantities of American weapons. In Britain too, millions of women were recruited to help the war effort. Along with building planes and tanks, and making shells and ammunition, women worked on farms, as mechanics at airbases and vehicle depots, and as doctors and nurses in military hospitals.

INTERNET LINK

For a link to websites where you can hear radio broadcasts, see video clips and discover more about daily life in Britain and the United States during the war, go to **www.usborne-quicklinks.com**

The good to bad life

In the first few years of the war, the Germans plundered their conquered territories, and German citizens enjoyed luxury goods in their shops. But, when the tide of the war turned against Germany, goods became scarce and the constant threat of bombing made life much more difficult. Hitler was still reluctant to allow German women to work in factories. This was partly due to Nazi attitudes to women, summed up by the pre-war slogan: *Children, Church and Kitchen*. The Nazis felt that these were the most suitable roles for women. So, although some German women worked in industry, much of the work was carried out by slave workers from prisoner-of-war camps or conquered peoples.

Gas attack

Most civilian populations expected to be bombed both by high explosives and gas. In Britain, people were expected to carry gas masks at all times. But, fortunately, gas was never used on civilians.

These British children are taking part in a gas mask drill in February 1941. They are all evacuees from London and are being looked after in Windsor, to the west of the capital.

Evacuation

The fear of bombing led to mass evacuation of children from British and German cities, as soon as war broke out - although Berlin itself was not evacuated until 1943. The Japanese also sent city children to live with families in the countryside. This spared many thousands of lives, as Japan's mainly wooden cities were bombed with merciless ferocity.

These schoolchildren evacuees are boarding a train to take them away from a Japanese city. The trip almost certainly saved their lives. Japan's cities were attacked with even greater savagery than Germany's.

THE WAR IN NORTH AFRICA

Between 1940 and 1943, the hot, sandy deserts and shores of North Africa became a crucial battlefield. From this desert war, two great generals emerged on opposing sides: Bernard Montgomery and Erwin Rommel. For them, the desert was a perfect place to wage war. There were very few towns and civilians to get in the way, and they could move their forces around almost like pieces on a chessboard.

Soldiers of the 8th Army, dug into makeshift stone and sand shelters, look on as Afrika Korps vehicles burn in the flat desert landscape.

Italy joins the war

In June 1940, Italy joined Germany in the war, and in September attacked British forces in Egypt. The British responded by launching successful attacks on Italy's African colonies: Libya, Ethiopia and Italian East Africa.

Rommel to the rescue

With his ally facing humiliation, Hitler sent German Afrika Korps troops to help, led by the formidable Erwin Rommel, fresh from victories in France. His resourcefulness and cunning earned him a nickname: *the Desert Fox*. Rommel compared fighting in the desert to fighting at sea, saying, "No admiral ever won a naval battle from the shore." He risked capture and death by directing battles right from the front line.

Successes and failures

Between 1940 and 1942, the desert war went back and forth over the north coast of Africa. After initial British successes, the Afrika Korps made a determined advance, gradually beating the British 8th Army back as far as the Egyptian border.

Rommel's new rival

In summer 1942, the exhausted and demoralized 8th Army was given a new commander, General Bernard Montgomery. "Monty" (as he was known) was eccentric and often rude. But he also had a gift for inspiring confidence in his troops.

Vichy 1940 - 42
Axis occupation
Allied occupation

ITALY
ALGERIA
MOROCCO
TUNISIA
Mediterranean Sea
LIBYA
El Alamein
EGYPT

Fighting took place along the whole of the North African coastline between 1940 to 1943. The Battle of El Alamein decided once and for all who would be the victor in the desert war.

"The Devil's Garden"

During the summer, both sides established strong defensive positions around the Egyptian town of El Alamein, near Alexandria. The Afrika Korps had surrounded themselves with so many deep minefields and booby traps, the area was known as the Devil's Garden.

By October 1942, Rommel had retired to Germany, ill with exhaustion. Most of his planes had been transferred east to fight the Soviets. On October 23, Montgomery launched a massive attack. It began with a thousand-gun bombardment, so intense the acting German commander suffered a fatal heart attack. Then, 230,000 8th Army troops and 1,230 tanks picked their way across the minefields to fight.

Rommel returned to find his army in a retreat that did not stop for 2,250km (1,400 miles). After the battle, British prime minister Winston Churchill commented, "...this is not the end. It is not even the beginning of the end. But it is, perhaps, the end of the beginning." This major British victory was followed by Allied landings in Morocco and Algeria in November. Caught between these two armies, the Afrika Korps surrendered in May 1943.

INTERNET LINK
For a link to a website where you can follow the battles in North Africa with animated maps, go to
www.usborne-quicklinks.com

LIFE IN OCCUPIED TERRITORIES

Like all empire builders, the Axis powers sought to exploit the resources - and the people - of the countries they conquered. As the war began to turn against them, they did so with increasing ruthlessness.

Bad company

In every conquered country, food and raw materials were taken at will. In Europe, the Nazis confiscated art and luxury goods - either for their own private collections, or to fill the shops at home. Road signs were written in German, even in Russia, which didn't even share the same alphabet. Nazi propaganda, in radio, cinema and street posters, became an inescapable fact of life.

The Nazis believed the people they conquered in the East were racially inferior. In Poland and parts of Russia, children with blonde hair and so-called "Aryan" looks were taken away to be brought up in Germany. Russians, who were regarded as little better than animals, were treated especially badly. They were addressed by a number, rather than by name, and made to wear that number on their clothes. Much worse was to follow. For example, when Soviet soldiers liberated the village of Parichi, near Bobruysk, they uncovered the bodies of children bled dry to provide blood transfusions for wounded German officers at a field hospital there.

Slave workers

Hundreds of thousands of people in eastern Europe and Russia were transported to Germany to work in armaments factories. Picked at random from towns and villages, they were whipped into cattle wagons or freight cars. If they survived the journey, they faced 18-hour days manufacturing tanks, aircraft or machine guns, for companies such as Daimler-Benz, Krupp and Siemens.

Japanese control

In the first six months of the war, Japan occupied over a million square miles (160 million km) of territory, with a population of over 150 million people. Unprepared for such staggering success, the Japanese relied on bullying and intimidation to control their new subject peoples. Everyone was ordered to bow to Japanese soldiers and officials. Those who did not risked anything from a slap in the face to decapitation. The Japanese language was taught in schools, and even the year was changed to fit in with the Japanese calendar - which made it 2602 instead of 1942.

This Eastern European recruitment poster, urges Croatian and Bosnian men to join the Nazi SS.

Nazi collaborators

Not everyone resented their new masters. There were many who cooperated with the Nazis - either for their own selfish reasons, or because they shared their anti-Semitic ideas. In most of the conquered nations, they helped round up local Jews. The SS recruited over 300,000 young men who were considered sufficiently "Aryan" to join them. In France, an auxiliary police force, the *Milice*, worked with the Germans to suppress the French Resistance.

Paris, during the German occupation of 1941-1944. This café, *La Place Blanche*, was reserved exclusively for the use of German soldiers.

THE BATTLE OF THE ATLANTIC

As the world's richest nation, the United States could produce more ships, planes and arms than any other country. This gave the Allies a great advantage. But, before they could be put to use, these weapons, and the men to fight with them, had to cross the Atlantic Ocean. For most of the war, the Atlantic was a bleak battleground between German submarines and Allied ships, in a desperate struggle for control of the supply route to Britain.

This map of the Atlantic shows in red where most ships were sunk by U-boats.

Convoys

British and other Allied merchant ships set off from North America in large groups known as convoys. They were protected by small warships - destroyers, corvettes and frigates - and, for some of their journey, by aircraft. The destroyers carried a detection device known as *asdic* - which used sound and its echo to locate submarines underwater.

Wolf packs

Waiting for them, especially as they neared the end of the journey, was a fearsome selection of German warships, aircraft and mines. But the greatest danger came from submarines, or U-boats, which roamed the Atlantic in groups known as wolf packs. They usually attacked on the surface, where asdic couldn't find them, and at night where they were less easily seen. The submarines used powerful cannon or torpedoes to sink the ships.

Life at sea

Life aboard a submarine was uncomfortable and dangerous. Men slept in bunks or hammocks right next to torpedoes or among engine room machinery. There were no facilities to shower or do laundry, and voyages could last six to eight weeks. Attacking convoys was such dangerous work that submariners called their vessels iron coffins.

Watery graves

For the first three years of the war, the U-boats were very successful. In a single night, October 18-19, 1940, for example, two convoys were attacked by six U-boats and 32 ships were sunk. In 1942, they claimed an average of 96 ships a month. The Allies couldn't afford such losses.

This photograph was probably taken from another U-boat, during a fierce storm in the North Atlantic. Men from the submarine crowd onto the conning tower, for a break away from the vessel's stifling interior.

INTERNET LINK
For a link to a website where you can play a game to lead a convoy across the Atlantic and outwit German U-boats, go to
www.usborne-quicklinks.com

Striking back

But the Allies fought back with new equipment and weapons. Escort ships were fitted with much-improved radar, which enabled them to detect U-boats on the surface. This was so effective that submarines were forced to attack from underwater - which was more difficult. New aircraft with a longer range were able to target U-boats out in the middle of the Atlantic. The Allies also managed to crack the secret code used by U-boats to reveal their positions. Forewarned of an attack, the convoys were able to defend themselves more effectively.

Ships by the yard

In March 1943, at the height of the so-called Battle of the Atlantic, U-boats sunk 105 Allied ships. But American shipyards were building 140 cargo ships a month, which enabled them to keep supplying their allies. The German navy, on the other hand, was being gradually worn down. Submarine losses were increasing, and new ones couldn't be built fast enough to replace them.

By 1944, when the Allies were preparing to invade France, the Battle of the Atlantic was almost over. Nearly two million soldiers and two million tons of military supplies had crossed the Ocean, with very few men lost. In the closing stages of the war, the average U-boat lasted only one or two missions before it was sunk. Nearly 1,200 U-boats fought in the war, and two out of three of them were sunk, with a loss of 30,000 out of 40,000 men.

A depth charge fired from an American escort destroyer

These lucky few German submariners have escaped from their sinking vessel and await rescue by a Canadian ship.

PROPAGANDA

Throughout the war, governments on both sides tried to present information about what was happening on the battlefronts, or in the conquered territories, in a way that would maintain support for them and the war. This is known as propaganda. The Axis powers often presented outright lies as straight news; the Allies were usually more truthful. But they, too, were happy to tell lies if it suited their purpose.

Passing on the message

Today many people get their news from television and the Internet, but neither was available at the time of the Second World War. Instead, public opinion was formed by newspapers and radio, as it still is today, and by newsreels - news shown in cinemas before the main film. Posters were also used to publicize a political message. On the front lines, all sides dropped leaflets on enemy forces, encouraging them to desert or surrender.

Controlling the media

Germany, Japan, Italy and the Soviet Union were all ruled by "totalitarian" governments, who exercised an iron grip over their people. This meant the media in these countries was totally controlled by the government, which had to approve every piece of news. It was not so tightly regulated in Britain, her empire, or in the United States - but editors were expected to judge for themselves what was "in the national interest" to pass on to the public.

This image showing the Nazi idea of the ideal "Aryan" German boy was used on a poster to recruit fire crews to combat the damage caused by air raids.

Jugend im Luftschutz!

Not afraid to use crude racial caricatures, this American poster warns home front workers to beware of enemy spies.

This American leaflet, dropped in China, shows an American airman trampling on a Japanese soldier.

This Soviet leaflet was distributed to Soviet soldiers. Under Hitler's orders, German troops are turned into Nazi swastikas and march to their graves.

Masters of propaganda

Nazi Propaganda Ministry chief, Dr. Joseph Goebbels, summed up his aim as, "to arouse outbursts of fury ... to organize hatred and suspicion - all with ice cold calculation." Germans were constantly reminded - by newsreels, radio broadcasts and newspapers - that communists and Jews were their greatest enemies, and that it was Germany's natural right to conquer land in the east. When the war turned against Germany, the job of the propagandists was made harder. After announcing Russia's defeat in 1941 and the fall of Stalingrad in 1942, they later had to acknowledge these stories had been false. Many Germans began to doubt the information their government gave them.

The Japanese crusade

The Japanese government told its citizens that its conquest of Pacific Asia was a crusade to liberate the east from European colonialists. When Japan occupied the Philippines, their radio claimed the locals had greeted them with cries of, "the angels are here!" The cruelty of the Japanese army, infamous for rape and massacre in conquered cities, was never mentioned.

Hitler the buffoon

The British and Americans told their own lies too, but never on the same scale. British newspapers tried to present the disaster at Dunkirk as a great victory. American propaganda slyly let on that Hitler's real name was the unattractive-sounding *Schicklegruber*. A newsreel showing a jubilant Hitler reacting to the news of the French surrender in June 1940 was doctored to look as if the Führer was dancing a delighted jig. The British people were encouraged to believe that Hitler was a maniac who chewed the carpet when he was angry. The purpose of such stories was to make the German leader look like a buffoon, rather than a formidable monster.

Truth or lies

The best propaganda simply told the truth. When German soldiers were transferred from France to fight at Stalingrad, Russian planes dropped leaflets, with a simple, chilling message: "Men of the 23rd Panzer Division, welcome to the Soviet Union. The gay Parisian life is now over. Your comrades will have told you what things are like here, but you will soon find out for yourselves."

THE HOLOCAUST

Map showing the location of the main Nazi death camps

Right from the start, the Nazis had reserved a special hatred for the Jews - blaming them for all of Germany's ills, especially defeat in the First World War and the economic upheavals that followed. Before war broke out in 1939, over 735,000 German and Austrian Jews suffered from fierce persecution, and the majority fled abroad. After the startling German victories at the beginning of the war, millions more Jews fell into the clutches of the Nazis.

A German firing squad executes Jewish men at Drohobycz, in Poland.

From migration to mass killing

The Nazis had always intended to drive the Jews from Germany and their conquered territories to make them *Judenfrei* - or *Jew-free*. At first, they thought this could be achieved by forced emigration to limited areas in Polish and Russian cities, known as *ghettos*. Another suggestion was that all the Jews might be herded off to a faraway island, such as Madagascar, off the coast of Africa. But, as the war progressed, this idea was increasingly seen as impractical.

Whenever the Germans conquered new territory in the east, squads of uniformed SS men, known as *Einsatzgruppen* (or Special Action Squads), would arrive in their wake to search for Jews. Some Jews were sent to a ghetto - but mostly they were killed, usually by being shot. In a mass killing, in September 1941, at Babi Yar, near Kiev in the Soviet Union, 33,000 Jews were shot over three days. By the end of the year, over a million Jews had been killed in such massacres.

The Final Solution

These random killings were time-consuming and messy, and difficult to keep secret from the local people - and the rest of the world. On January 20, 1942, Nazi leaders decided on a more efficient way of eliminating Jews. At the Wannsee Conference, held in a villa outside Berlin, it was decided to send all Jews in Nazi territory to special death camps, to be gassed to death. This was known as *die Endlösung* - the Final Solution.

Acting directly on the orders of Hitler and the head of the SS, Heinrich Himmler, the Final Solution was masterminded by SS General Reinhard Heydrich, and the head of the *Gestapo* Jewish Affairs Section, Adolf Eichmann. Death camps were built in Poland, which had the densest Jewish population in Europe. Plans were drawn up to transport millions of people to the camps in freight trucks and cattle wagons.

The head of the SS - Reichsmarshal Heinrich Himmler.

Nightmare journey

From Norway to the Caucusus, Jews were rounded up and packed into freight trains. Many died on the journey, from lack of food or water, and disease. In some camps, such as Auschwitz, they were split into two groups - those who would be worked to death, and those who would be killed at once. In other camps, such as Belzec, Sobibor and Treblinka, Jews were killed as soon as they arrived.

Revolt and rebellion

Jews sent to the death camps were told they were going to be "resettled" - but, after a few succeeded in escaping, the terrible truth reached others outside. A small group left in the ghetto in Warsaw, the Polish capital, rose up in rebellion. They managed to fight off the Germans for almost a month - from April 19 to May 16, 1943.

But the rebellion was crushed and the deportations continued. In Sobibor, 600 Jews tried to escape; 300 survived and joined the local partisans. In October, 1943, nearly all Denmark's 6,000 Jews were smuggled out to neutral Sweden, when it was discovered that the Nazis intended to deport them. But these were only tiny victories. It is estimated that between five and a half and six million Jews died in what became known as the Holocaust.

> " The Führer has ordered that the Jewish question be settled once and for all... Every Jew that we lay our hands on has to be destroyed. "

Heinrich Himmler in conversation with Rudolf Höss, the commandant of Auschwitz, in the summer of 1941.

AUSCHWITZ-BIRKENAU

Busiest of all death camps was the vast complex of Auschwitz-Birkenau, near the Polish town of Auschwitz. Between the summer of 1942 and the last days of 1944, perhaps more than a million people were murdered there. The site had been chosen because it was at the heart of the Nazi empire, and had excellent rail connections - ideal for transporting Jews from all over the conquered territories.

From this photo of Auschwitz-Birkenau, you can see just how huge the camp was. The long dark strip on the left was where arriving Jews were deposited from the trains and selected for work or immediate extermination. It was known as *the ramp*.

A glimpse into hell

The aerial photograph on the right shows Auschwitz-Birkenau at 11am on August 25, 1944, when the last Polish Jews from the Lodz ghetto were being gassed. It is estimated that around 437,000 Hungarian Jews had been killed here earlier that summer. On the far side of the photograph, you can just make out smoke from a burial pit. This was where bodies were dumped to be burned, when the camp crematoria were overloaded.

The ramp

Trains ran directly into the camp, and arrivals were subjected to "selection" by officers and doctors. The fittest and strongest were placed on one side. The rest - the sick, the old, and women with their children - were chosen for immediate extermination. In the picture below, those on the left are heading for the gas chamber. Those on the right will become slave workers, and survive for a few months more.

New arrivals at Auschwitz-Birkenau have just disembarked from their cattle trucks, and are being "selected" by German officers. You can identify the other inmates by their characteristic striped uniforms.

The gas chambers

Those selected for death were told they were being sent to a shower block - which was actually a large gas chamber located next to a crematorium. There were four main gas chambers and crematorium facilities at Auschwitz-Birkenau. Victims were herded into the chamber, hundreds at a time, then poisoned with a cyanide gas called Zyklon B.

"Canada"

The people who had been chosen to die were disposed of with typical Nazi efficiency. Their heads were shaved and the hair was used for insulation in aircraft and submarines. Clothes, shoes, spectacles, suitcases and other belongings were sent to Germany. Gold teeth and wedding rings were removed and melted down. After cremation, the ashes were used as fertilizer. A section of the camp near the gas chambers was used for storage. With ghoulish irony, the inmates named it "Canada" - a land of plenty and prosperity.

A pile of shoes, taken from victims of the gas chambers

Liberation day

As the Red Army approached from the East, 67,000 of the camp's dwindling inhabitants were rounded up and marched back to Germany. When the Soviets finally arrived on January 27, 1945, they found around 2,800 sick and frail survivors.

These ragged inmates were photographed by a Soviet journalist when Auschwitz was liberated in January, 1945.

INTERNET LINK
For a link to a website where you can take a virtual tour of Auschwitz, go to **www.usborne-quicklinks.com**

53

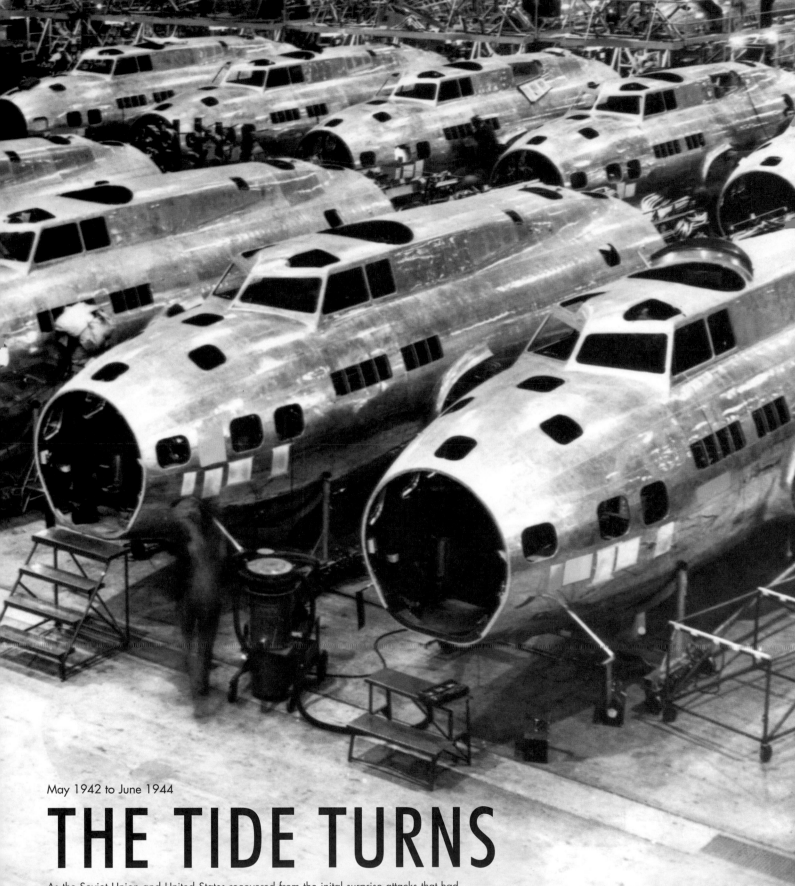

May 1942 to June 1944

THE TIDE TURNS

As the Soviet Union and United States recovered from the inital surprise attacks that had brought them into the war, they began to harness their huge industrial power to produce weapons to enable them to win it. America's ability to produce more tanks, aircraft, ships and guns than any other nation ensured the Allied victory. Here, rows of *B-17 Flying Fortresses* are being made ready for the air war in Europe, at a Boeing factory in Seattle, Washington.

CORAL SEA AND MIDWAY

In the spring of 1942, Japan was at the height of its power. Its assault on the Pacific was so successful, that plans were now laid for the invasion of Australia via New Guinea, and Hawaii via the island of Midway. Meantime, the US Navy was making a determined recovery from Pearl Harbor. The Japanese were about to discover the true potential of their formidable enemy.

Separated by thousands of miles of ocean, the battles at Coral Sea and Midway stopped Japan in its tracks.

America hits back

The overall damage inflicted at Pearl Harbor could have been much worse. Only two of the 18 warships hit were totally destroyed; within six months the rest were refloated and repaired. Better still, three aircraft carriers - the most important ships stationed at Pearl Harbor - had been out at sea during the attack - and escaped without a scratch.

Like all navies, the Japanese ships communicated with each other, and their high command, using secret code. But the Americans had broken this code. They found out that a large Japanese fleet was preparing to invade the southern tip of New Guinea, and they prepared an ambush.

Making history

In the Battle of the Coral Sea, on May 4-8, 1942, neither fleet actually set eyes on each other. For the first time in history, all the fighting was done by planes from aircraft carriers. Two valuable Japanese aircraft carriers were put out of action; several other warships and around 100 carrier planes were lost. The United States lost one aircraft carrier, two other ships, and 65 planes. The battle was inconclusive, but it seriously halted the Japanese advance. From now on, there would be a slow retreat back to Japan.

Meeting at Midway

The following month brought another trial of strength. A Japanese fleet of 145 ships, including eight aircraft carriers and 11 battleships, was heading for the American island of Midway. They were commanded by Admiral Yamamoto, who hoped to draw the American fleet into a decisive battle. But, once again, Japanese radio messages were intercepted, and the Americans were waiting.

On June 4, 1942, US aircraft launched a massive attack on the Japanese fleet, both from US aircraft carriers and airfields at Midway. The Japanese fought back. But Yamamoto had split his massive invasion force into small groups, and fatally underestimated American naval strength. It was to be his undoing.

Five minutes that changed the world

Around 10:30 in the morning, in what might have been the most momentous five minutes of the war, three Japanese aircraft carriers were destroyed. Another was badly damaged and sank later in the day, as well as two cruisers and three destroyers. The Americans lost an aircraft carrier, *Yorktown*, and a single destroyer. Again, neither fleet actually saw each other. All the fighting was done from the air.

The Battle of Midway was the turning point in the Pacific War. The Japanese navy had been fatally undermined - and her expansion plans were postponed. From now on, the US Navy would be the dominant power in the Pacific.

INTERNET LINK
For a link to a website where you can see film footage and a slide show of the Battle of the Coral Sea, go to
www.usborne-quicklinks.com

Men abandon the US aircraft carrier *Lexington*, during the Battle of the Coral Sea. Amazingly, not one life was lost during the evacuation of the ship.

THE BATTLE OF STALINGRAD

In June 1942, the German army lurched deep into the south of Russia. In the summer heat, with the vast Russian Steppe baked hard beneath their tank tracks and truck wheels, they swept forward in a great cloud of dust. By August they had reached the Caucusus Mountains, and the suburbs of Stalingrad. Defended by a ragged force only half their size, the Germans were convinced the city would fall in little more than a day.

A model city

Previously known as Tsaritsyn, Stalingrad had been renamed after the Soviet leader, because he had defended it in the Russian Civil War. It was a major transport hub, with important factories and steel works, and a population of 500,000, spread out 32km (20 miles) along the banks of the Volga. Leading the German attack was General Friedrich von Paulus, commander of the 200,000 men and 500 tanks of the 6th Army and 4th Panzer Army. Facing him was General Vasily Chuikov, commander of the 50,000 strong Soviet 62nd Army. On August 23, tanks and infantry began their first probing attacks on the outskirts of Stalingrad, while 600 *Luftwaffe* bombers attacked the city. Over 40,000 civilians were killed on that first day.

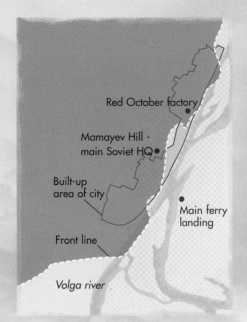

Stalingrad in September 1942, showing some of the key places in the battle. The red area is occupied by the Germans.

Brutal battleground

By late September, the city was nearly in German hands. But the fighting was extremely brutal, and the Russians showed no sign of giving up. Most of Stalingrad had been reduced to rubble, but it created perfect cover for the defenders. The Germans had to fight for the city room by room - rather than street by street. Chuikov told his men that every soldier was his own general - free to fight as best he could in the ruins of the city.

Breaking point

By early October, Chuikov had lost thousands of men and was under such stress he had developed painful eczema on his hands. Von Paulus, who had expected a quick victory, now had an uncontrollable tic in one eye. He launched a final all-out assault on the tangled remains of factories and steelworks in the industrial area of the city. But the Russians had been strengthened by reinforcements and were prepared. The assault failed.

Counter attack

By now the German 6th Army was exhausted. Winter was fast approaching, and the troops were ill-equipped for cold weather fighting. Outside the city, a million Soviet troops, with strong artillery, tank and aircraft support, prepared to counterattack. The ground where they decided to strike was well chosen. It was held by soldiers of Germany's allies: Italy, Rumania and Hungary. Unlike the well-trained, battle-hardened German troops, these men had no desire to be in Russia at all. Once, when a whole battalion of Italians had surrendered without firing a shot, a Soviet interpreter asked why they hadn't fought. "We did not fire back because we thought it would be a mistake," replied a sergeant.

INTERNET LINK
For a link to a website where you can see photographs taken during the Battle of Stalingrad, go to
www.usborne-quicklinks.com

In sharp winter sunshine, Soviet troops advance through the ruins of Stalingrad.

59

THE DEATH OF AN ARMY

The Soviet counterattack came from both north and south of Stalingrad - cutting through with ease the Italian and Rumanian armies who were defending territory outside the city. In less than a week, the Soviet armies met up in the village of Sovietsky. Von Paulus and 250,000 German, Rumanian and Croatian soldiers were surrounded.

Plea to retreat

Von Paulus immediately sent a message to Hitler, asking for permission to get out of Stalingrad before his army was destroyed. He could not have been franker: "Army heading for disaster. It is essential to withdraw all our divisions…"

But while Hitler and his generals discussed von Paulus's predicament, they were joined by the vain and bombastic head of the *Luftwaffe*, Hermann Goering. He convinced Hitler that the vast quantities of fuel, food and ammunition needed by the German 6th Army could be supplied by air to two airfields just outside the city. Von Paulus was told to hold fast, and so began the agonizing disintegration of his exhausted army.

Desperate failure

Goering's plan was a disaster. He didn't have enough planes to carry the supplies, and what planes he had were being reduced in number every day by Soviet fighters. Freezing fog often prevented flying and, even on the best days, only half the supplies needed arrived at the two airfields. Thousands of badly wounded men, awaiting a flight back to Germany, froze to death in flimsy tents alongside the runways.

Hitler ordered one of his best generals, Field Marshal Erich von Manstein, to break through the Soviet forces to open up a corridor to supply the 6th Army. His forces attacked from the south on December 12, 1942.

While the attack was diverting the Russian army, von Paulus again asked Hitler for permission to break out. He was refused. By December 23, it was clear that von Manstein had failed. The Soviet forces now surrounding Stalingrad were too strong.

Unhappy Christmas

Von Paulus's army was doomed. On Christmas Day alone, nearly 1,300 men died from frostbite, starvation and disease. The Soviet forces sensed victory, and harried them mercilessly. In January, the Soviets offered generous surrender terms. Von Paulus's men were roaming the streets, desperately searching for food and warmth. He also had 20,000 wounded soldiers in need of medical attention - but, incredibly, his loyalty to Hitler made him refuse. And so the battle dragged on.

The battle lost, von Paulus and other German commanders surrender to the Soviets. The agony of their futile struggle shows on their faces.

> INTERNET LINK
> For a link to a website where you can listen to reports from Stalingrad as the Germans surrendered, go to
> **www.usborne-quicklinks.com**

Soviet troops attack German positions, deep in the ruins of the "Red October" metalworks factory in Stalingrad.

Promotion and ruin

With the battle almost over, Hitler promoted von Paulus to the rank of Field Marshal. No German Field Marshal had ever been captured, so this was a strong hint that von Paulus should commit suicide. He didn't. He was captured on January 31; the 6th Army surrendered on February 2.

As an unaccustomed silence fell over the city, Russian soldiers began to fire captured German signal flares into the air, and bright reds and greens lit up the smoking ruins of the city. Stalingrad lay in ruins: 41,000 homes, 300 factories, 113 schools and hospitals - 99% of its buildings - had been destroyed. But a great Russian victory had been won. The German defeat at Stalingrad would later be seen as the greatest turning point of the war.

THE SECRET WAR

Knowing what your enemy is going to do is a priceless asset for a military commander. During battles, armies use reconnaissance patrols and aircraft to try to discover what the other side is doing. But it's even better to know in advance what the enemy intends to do. Codebreakers, spies and informants can provide this information - often at great personal risk. But the world of espionage is dark and cunning, and what appears to be vital information can turn out to have been deliberately planted by the enemy to mislead...

Their man in Tokyo

Plans for many of the greatest battles of the war were reported by spies before they happened. Richard Sorge was a German journalist who worked for the German embassy in Tokyo. But, unfortunately for the Germans, Sorge was secretly working for the Soviets, and was sending frequent reports back to Moscow.

When Sorge discovered that the Germans intended to attack the Soviet Union in autumn 1941 - but that Japan had no intention of joining them - the Russians were able to transfer crack army divisions from their eastern border to their western front line. This ensured that the Soviet Union was saved from defeat. Sorge also warned them about the Pearl Harbor attack, but the Russians didn't pass on the information to the United States. He was arrested in November 1941, and executed in 1944.

This is the Japanese identification document carried by Richard Sorge.

Enemies in both camps

Rudolph Rössler (codenamed "Lucy") was a Swiss citizen with several German military friends who detested their own Nazi government. They sent Rössler a constant stream of information which he sometimes passed on to the Allies. The invasions of Denmark and Norway, German tactics during the invasion of France, *Operation Barbarossa*, and subsequent Nazi campaigns in Russia, all came through "Lucy".

The Germans had a spy in Turkey - codenamed "Cicero" - who was the manservant of the British Ambassador there. He spied for money and passed on to the Nazis details of the Normandy Landings. He was paid in forged banknotes. Luckily for the Allies, his reports were disbelieved.

An amazing coincidence

Intelligence organizations can sometimes be too cautious. In May, 1944, a crossword compiler for the *Daily Telegraph* was interrogated by two intelligence officers, on suspicion of being a spy. In the month before the D-Day landings, his crossword had contained several secret codewords relating to the invasion: *Utah*, and *Omaha* (the two American landing spots), *Mulberry* (the makeshift piers to be used on the beaches) and *Neptune* (the naval operation on D-Day). Eventually they accepted that it was just an extraordinary coincidence. The full story only emerged in 1984. The crossword compiler was a teacher who had asked his pupils to suggest words. One of his pupils lived next to a camp of soldiers making ready for the invasion and had picked up the words by evesdropping on their conversations.

The world of espionage is full of twists and turns, and it is easy to make mistakes, as British Intelligence showed when they interrogated the compiler of the *Daily Telegraph* crossword.

INTERNET LINK

For a link to a website where you can try sending secret messages using a virtual ENIGMA machine and learn some codebreaking tricks, go to **www.usborne-quicklinks.com**

Codebreakers

Any message sent by radio can be picked up by an enemy listening in, so throughout the war both sides used codes. Perhaps the most difficult one to crack was the German ENIGMA code, which was constantly being updated. But, thanks to the extraordinary efforts of Polish and British codebreakers, for most of the war the Allies were able to uncover some of the German plans in advance. The war in North Africa, the Battle of the Atlantic, the invasion of Sicily and Italy, and the Normandy Landings were all Allied victories won with the help of ENIGMA codebreakers. The Americans broke Japanese codes too, enabling them to intercept Japanese naval forces during the crucial Battle of Midway in 1942, and to shoot down a plane carrying Admiral Yamamoto in 1943.

German codebreakers also cracked the British codes used to transmit convoy routes. In 1942, 2,000 convoy signals a month were being picked up by the German navy and passed on to U-boat commanders searching for targets. The code was changed when the British discovered it had been broken.

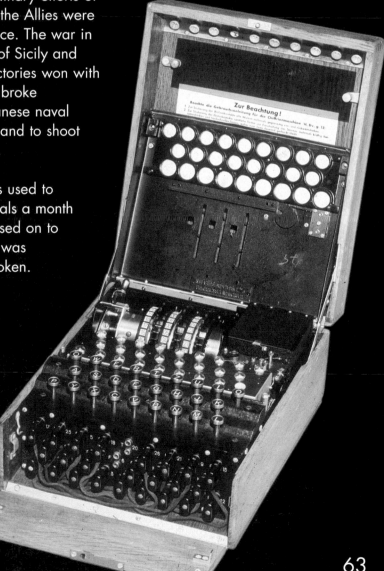

Bletchley Park, Buckinghamshire, where British Intelligence translated German signals encoded by the ENIGMA machine, shown here on the right.

KURSK

In the winter months after Stalingrad, the German army fought to regain its momentum. In March 1943, the Germans recaptured the Soviet city of Kharkov. Then another great opportunity presented itself. A huge bulge in the front line around the city of Kursk offered them the chance to enclose and destroy three Soviet army groups at once. A victory like that might turn the war on the Eastern Front to Germany's advantage once more.

The Germans tried to link up at Kursk. The red shaded areas show how far they got.

Another gamble

The attack on Kursk came with great risks. At this stage of the war, the armies on both sides were equally matched. But the Soviets were now beginning to overtake the Axis forces with tanks, artillery and aircraft. Still, Hitler had owed his military success so far to a series of audacious gambles, so perhaps he would succeed again at Kursk?

New tanks

The attack could have taken place in early spring, but German commanders decided to wait for the arrival of two powerful new tanks: the *Panther* and the *Tiger*. More able to withstand direct hits, with more powerful guns, these new models promised to annihilate the standard Soviet tank - the *T-34*.

Despite these advantages, when describing the imminent assault on Kursk to his Eastern Front commanders, Hitler complained, *"Whenever I think of this attack, my stomach turns over."*

A fatal delay

Their tanks in place, the Germans began their assault on July 5. But, in the weeks before the attack, the Soviets had been busy. Informed by spies that an attack was coming, they had reinforced their positions with deep minefields, 20,000 extra field guns and over a thousand *Katyusha* rocket launchers. The clash that followed would be the greatest tank battle in history.

Soviet tanks and soldiers prepare to launch an assault during the Battle of Kursk.

Making history

In the flat grasslands of Central Russia, 6,000 tanks, 5,000 aircraft and two million men fought to win control of the war. This small section of the front contained more than the entire fighting force in Western Europe over 1944-45. As the tanks trundled towards each other, the sky was filled with opposing aircraft. The Soviet air force, having recovered from virtual annihilation in the first days of the war, flew 28,000 missions over the battlefield.

All-out carnage

The battle raged for eight days, most of the time in torrential rain. The carnage was horrific: about 90,000 men were killed or wounded. The Soviets lost over 2,300 tanks, the Germans around 400. The German tanks had been alarmingly effective, and more difficult to destroy, but they suffered breakdowns and other problems which blunted their usefulness.

Sunk in despair, a dead comrade sprawled behind him, this German soldier was photographed by his Soviet captors during the fighting in Kursk. German forces were completely outnumbered by the Soviets.

INTERNET LINK

For a link to a website where you can see photographs taken at the Battle of Kursk, go to **www.usborne-quicklinks.com**

Diversion from the south

For all the Soviet losses, the Germans could not penetrate their deep defensive positions. Soviet tanks were quickly replaced. Five days into the battle, another one began thousands of miles away, when British and American troops invaded Sicily. Hitler ordered an immediate transfer of some of the forces from Kursk. After a few more days, it became clear the Germans had failed. From this moment, the war would be one long retreat back to Berlin.

Scorched Earth

Immensely destructive fighting like this caused such damage that, by the end of the war, the Soviet Union had lost about 30% of its entire wealth. In retreat, both sides destroyed anything they could that might be useful to the enemy. This desperate tactic was known as *Scorched Earth*.

ALLIED BOMBING IN EUROPE

Until the beginning of the 20th century, wars were waged between opposing armies on the ground. But in the Second World War, the use of bomber aircraft led to the deaths of thousands of civilians, hundreds of miles from the front lines. The war began with squadrons of German bombers laying waste to city districts. But, from 1942, British and American aircraft were able to destroy entire German cities in massive thousand bomber raids.

Allied strategy

When US forces began to arrive in Britain in 1942, plans were made for a great bomber offensive against Germany. The British specialized in lumbering night bombers, such as the *Lancaster*, *Halifax* and *Stirling,* which attacked cities in a tactic known as area bombing. Their aim was to "dehouse" the German population, and undermine civilian support for the Nazis and the war.

The Americans had more heavily armed, better protected bombers, such as the *B-17 Flying Fortress* and the *B-24 Liberator*. These were used in daytime attacks to bomb specific industrial and military targets, such as factories or railway yards. "The more *Flying Fortresses* we have, the shorter the war is going to be," said a US Air Force commander, Curtis LeMay. But it wasn't that simple.

This drifting black smoke is caused by anti-aircraft shells set to explode at the same height as the bombers.

Heavy losses

Heavy bombers such as the *Flying Fortress* were very expensive - $250,000 each - but they were highly vulnerable to both day and night fighters. German anti-aircraft fire was often radar-controlled and very accurate. The US lost over 8,000 heavy bombers and about 40,000 men. On one raid alone, against ball-bearing manufacturing plants in Schweinfurt, Germany, in October 1943, 60 of the 300 bombers sent on the mission were shot down. At the height of the war, RAF losses averaged 10% a raid - a chilling statistic for bomber crews who had to complete 30 missions before they could be reassigned to noncombat postings.

A squadron of *B-17 Flying Fortress* bombers is flying somewhere over Europe, on March 20, 1944.

Maximum impact?

The losses only began to decline with the introduction in 1944 of long-range fighter escorts, such as the *P-51 Mustang*. But the effects of the bombing campaign are more difficult to calculate. Rather than destroying civilian morale, the bombing raids actually increased support for the Nazis. The aircrews were called "Terror Fliers" by German propaganda. Like the British during the Blitz, the bombed German people were determined to carry on in defiance.

The bombing had a limited effect on the production of weapons in Germany, which continued to rise throughout 1944. But what the campaign did do was to divert much-needed resources away from the German front lines. By 1944, a quarter of all German artillery

A British pilot prepares for takeoff in a Lancaster bomber. Unlike most American bombers, which had a pilot and co-pilot, British bombers had only one pilot.

and ammunition was being used against Allied bombers. More importantly, almost all the remaining strength of the *Luftwaffe* was diverted to defending Germany's skies. This left German soldiers on all fronts with very little air support.

INTERNET LINK
For a link to a website where you can watch a movie that combines animations, photographs and audio clips, to get a glimpse of what it was like to be in a bomber and one of the bombed, go to
www.usborne-quicklinks.com

BOMBS

War always speeds up scientific and technological progress - and the Second World War was no exception. In 1939 bombs carried by bombers were the main method of attacking enemy cities from the air. But by 1945 pilotless missiles and rockets had been developed to do this.

Different shapes and sizes

Throughout the war, bombers dropped simple high-explosive bombs, similar in design to the ones used in the First World War. The German *Luftwaffe* dropped 1,800kg (4,000lb) bombs on Warsaw and London, which detonated when they hit the ground. The blast from the explosion could knock down an entire building. Bombers also dropped incendiary bombs. These burst into flame when they landed, setting fire to buildings.

A lone firefighter tries to extinguish the flames in a street in Narvik, Norway, which was destroyed by German incendiary bombs in April, 1940.

INTERNET LINK

For a link to a website where you can watch video clips of V weapons being launched and in flight, go to
www.usborne-quicklinks.com

Incendiary and high explosive bombs rain down from US B-29 bombers in July, 1945. Their target is the docks in the Japanese city of Kobe.

Rocket science

Near the end of the war, German scientists invented two new kinds of missiles, aimed at London and southern England, called the *V-1* and *V-2*. (The "V" stood for *Vengeance*.) The *V-1* was *a* pilotless missile, which carried an explosive warhead and flew like a plane. It was powered by a jet engine, which cut out when it reached its target, and the missile plummeted to Earth. *V-1*s flew slow enough for fighter planes to shoot them down.

Even more deadly

The *V-2* also carried an explosive warhead - but it was much deadlier than the *V-1*. Its rocket engine took it high into the atmosphere, and it came crashing down to Earth at great speed. The *V-2* flew faster than sound, so it would explode without warning, before anyone heard it coming. 1,115 of these rockets were launched on London, killing 2,754 and wounding more than twice that number.

This *V-2* rocket dwarfs the group of German technicians surrounding it. The development of weapons like this led directly to the exploration of space in the 1950s and 1960s.

BOMBERS

During wartime, weapon designers constantly try to keep one step ahead of the enemy. Improvements, which might take decades during peacetime, speed up considerably. Here are two of the most widely used bombers of the Second World War.

Most of the crew in the *Heinkel He-111* sat in the cabin at the front. It was unpressurized, so the crew had to wear oxygen masks.

Heinkel He-111

The German *Heinkel He -111* bomber was designed to support troops on the ground, and to fly short-range missions behind enemy lines. It had a crew of five, and was used extensively against Poland and Britain during 1939-1940. The plane had a range of 2,000km (1,243 miles) and could fly at 7,800m (25,590ft).

The two engines gave a top speed of 415kmph (258mph).

1,497kgs (3,300lbs) of bombs could be carried in the bomb bay between the wings.

Boeing B-29 Superfortress

The American *Boeing B-29 Superfortress* was designed to fly long-range missions to attack enemy cities. It had a crew of 10, a range of almost 6,000km (3,700 miles) and could fly at 11,018m (36,150ft). It was used to bomb Japan between 1944 and 1945.

Four engines gave a top speed of 575kmph (357mph).

INTERNET LINK

For a link to a website where you can watch a video clip of *B-29s* in flight and take a virtual tour of the plane, go to **www.usborne-quicklinks.com**

The tail gunner operated a powerful cannon.

The gunners sat here.

This is one of the seven single machine guns, or cannons, that protected the *Heinkel* from enemy fighters.

Happy landings

One major breakthrough in aircraft design was to place a wheel at the nose rather than the tail. This gave the pilot a much better view on takeoff and landing. The two small illustrations below are drawn to scale, so you can see how much bigger the *B-29* is compared to the *He-111*.

The silhouette of a *He-111*

Tail wheel

The silhouette of a *B-29*

Nose wheel

Ten machine guns and one cannon, placed on top and underneath the aircraft, protected the *B-29* from enemy fighters. Most of the machine guns were operated by remote control.

9,072kgs (20,000lbs) of bombs could be carried in two bomb bays in the undercarriage.

The pilots, engineer, bomb aimer and radio operator sat here. The compartments were pressurized, so members of the crew did not have to wear oxygen masks.

BATTLE OF THE TITANS

For nearly a hundred years, the heavily-armed battleship had been the world's most powerful weapon. All the major fighting nations in the war had their own fleets. But now there was a new arrival in the navy arsenal: the aircraft carrier. Carrying up to a hundred aircraft each, the carrier proved to be more than a match for even the mightiest battleship.

INTERNET LINK
For a link to a website with photographs of aircraft carriers from the Second World War, go to
www.usbornequicklinks.com

Big is best

The most powerful battleships ever built were two identical Japanese ships named *Yamato* and *Musashi*. Designed in the late 1930s, these titans of the sea weighed 71,000 tons each, were 263m (862ft) long, with a crew of 2,500. The *Yamato* was the flagship of the Japanese fleet, from which the commander-in-chief directed battle. It had three main gun turrets, each containing three guns which fired massive shells 45cm (18 inches) wide. It also carried another 24 smaller guns, and 146 anti-aircraft guns.

Apart from this extraordinary firepower, the *Yamato* was shielded by a 40cm (16 inch) protective layer of thick steel, with over a thousand watertight compartments to stop water from flooding through the ship. *Yamato* fought at the battles of Midway and Leyte Gulf and was eventually destroyed in April 1945, on the way to defend the Japanese island of Okinawa. It took eleven torpedoes and seven bombs to send this great ship to the bottom of the East China Sea. Significantly, these were delivered by a force of 179 aircraft, from nine American carriers.

The great battleship *Yamato*. Each of her three big gun turrets weighed more than a destroyer.

A new kind of warfare

Aircraft carriers had first been built during the First World War, but it was only in this war that they were put into action. British and US carriers were used to protect their convoys from enemy submarines and warships. Aircraft from the British *Ark Royal* weakened the powerful German battleship *Bismarck* and enabled the British to catch and sink it.

But it was in the Pacific that aircraft carriers proved most crucial. The attack on Pearl Harbor would have been inconceivable without them, as would the American campaign to oust the Japanese from their Pacific conquests. In a single day in July 1945, US carrier aircraft destroyed a battleship, three aircraft carriers, a cruiser and twelve other ships.

Planes on the crowded flight deck of *USS Hornet* have their wings folded to allow them to be stored below.

Floating towns

Typical of the US carriers used in the Pacific was *USS Essex,* which could carry up to 100 planes. There were 24 similar carriers built during the war. Because aircraft carriers were so deadly, they were the principal target of enemy attack, and had to be surrounded by an escort of battleships, cruisers and destroyers. Preparing an attack from a carrier was an immensely complex operation, involving a crew of 3,500. Planes had to be filled with fuel, armed with machine-gun bullets, bombs and torpedoes, and taken from hangers inside the carrier and up to the flight deck. Heavy torpedo bombers were placed at the stern, to give them the greatest length of deck to take off from.

WOMEN ON THE FRONT LINE

During the Second World War, women were killed in greater numbers than in any previous war - as victims of bombing, resistance reprisal massacres or in extermination camps. But in places where the war was fought with the fiercest determination, many women took an active role, becoming combatants too.

Abandoning traditional roles

Millions of women, especially in the Allied nations, made an invaluable contribution to the war effort by working in factories producing tanks, aircraft and munitions. But women were also employed near, or actually on, the front line. Thousands of female nurses worked in field hospitals close behind the fighting, where they could be victims of artillery or air attack. Even in Germany, where the Nazi Party disapproved of women taking on traditionally male roles, teenage girls manned the anti-aircraft guns aimed at the British and American bombers. Women also took on jobs as engineers, repairing aircraft, tanks and trucks, and as air raid wardens and ambulance crews.

Three Allied nurses tend to a wounded soldier near the front line in France, August 1944. Women did not usually take part in combat on the Western Front, but were still close enough to the fighting to be killed.

An air raid warden rescues a young girl from the wreckage of a London building bombed by the Germans during the Blitz.

Resistance fighters

The British and Americans didn't expect women to fight in combat, but the British made an exception with those who volunteered for the Special Operations Executive (SOE). This was a branch of the British secret service which trained agents to fight alongside men and women in resistance groups in Nazi-occupied Europe. One of them was Odette Sanson, a French woman living in London when the war broke out. She landed in the south of France in 1942 to assist French Resistance fighters in the area. Odette was captured, but managed to deceive the Germans into thinking she was married to a relative of Winston Churchill's. This did not stop her from being tortured, but it almost certainly saved her from execution - a fate that befell several other SOE women who were captured by the Nazis.

Soviet women fighters

On the Eastern Front, Soviet women were unavoidably much closer to the war than their contemporaries in Britain and America. As the Germans approached Moscow and Leningrad, thousands of women and children were transported to the outskirts to dig massive anti-tank ditches. Soviet women worked as medical assistants or radio operators right on the front lines, and fought as combat soldiers - dying alongside their male comrades in tanks and trenches. Polish women also fought with men in the Warsaw Uprising in summer 1944, and others took part in bitter partisan and guerrilla campaigns behind the Eastern Front.

This Russian girl, parachuted behind enemy lines, has just been captured by German soldiers. She faces certain execution.

Air aces

Early in the war the Soviets were losing pilots at a rate of 50% a year, so women were allowed to join the air force too. By the end of the war, over one in ten Soviet combat pilots were women. There were three all-female air regiments, flying fighters and bombers, with their own female ground crews to fuel, arm and repair their planes. There were mixed squadrons too. Lilya Litvak flew with her lover Alexei Salomaten, until he was killed in combat. She destroyed 11 or 12 aircraft before she was shot down by German fighters sent to hunt for her.

A Soviet woman pilot poses proudly next to her fighter plane.

INTERNET LINK

For a link to a website where you can read fascinating stories about women secret agents, go to **www.usborne-quicklinks.com**

ISLAND FIGHTING

In the summer of 1942, Allied troops began the troublesome task of clawing back the territory seized by Japan in the first six months of the Pacific War. Early battles suggested the Japanese would fight fanatically to hold on to what land they had captured, in the hope of reaching a compromise with their more powerful enemy. In the savage fighting that followed over the next three years - on sandy beaches and in dense, torrid jungles - tiny, unheard-of islands would earn an infamous place in the history of the Second World War.

The blue arrows show the two-pronged American assault against the Japanese. The area shaded dark blue shows the limits of Japan's new empire.

Operation Cartwheel

The Allied plan to reconquer the Pacific was a two-pronged assault known as *Operation Cartwheel*. General Douglas MacArthur led one prong, through New Guinea and on to the Philippines. The second, led by Admiral Chester Nimitz, was heading for Japan via the tiny islands of the central Pacific: the Marshall Islands, the Marianas, Iwo Jima and Okinawa.

Avoiding trouble

The Allies had much stronger naval and air forces, which allowed them to cut off supplies to Japanese strongpoints. So, wherever possible, Japanese garrisons were bypassed - left, as Chester Nimitz famously remarked, "to wither on the vine." The 100,000 strong Japanese force, at Rabaul in the Solomon Islands, was one example.

Guadalcanal

Following the US naval victories at Coral Sea and Midway, the Marines launched their first land assault, at Guadalcanal, in the Solomon Islands. Here the Japanese were building a large airbase, which would give them the potential to disrupt shipping between the USA, Australia and New Zealand.

Australian troops also joined in the fighting, which lasted from August 1942 to February 1943. Both sides suffered heavy casualties, but the Allies had more equipment and soldiers. Throughout the war, this gave them a decisive edge against their opponents.

As soon as the land fighting began, the Japanese soldiers proved both determined and ruthless. When they were certain of defeat, most would kill themselves rather than surrender. At Guadalcanal, wounded Japanese soldiers waited for American medics to attend to them, then blew themselves and their helpers to pieces with hand grenades.

Tarawa Atoll

To the south, across a vast swathe of empty ocean, lay Tarawa Atoll, a chain of small but heavily-fortified islands. In November 1943, on one of these islands - a narrow strip just four miles long, named Betio - 5,000 Japanese defenders fought to the last 17 men against invading US Marines. The Americans suffered 3,000 casualties in three days, with a thousand of them dying on the island.

INTERNET LINK
For a link to a website where you can watch film footage and see photographs of the Battle of Tarawa, go to
www.usborne-quicklinks.com

Under attack from Japanese machine-gun fire, American soldiers wade towards a beach on Makim Atoll, in the Gilbert Islands, during November 1943.

A different climate

In spring 1943, US troops invaded the island of Attu, in the Aleutians. Attu was Japan's most northerly conquest, and the fighting took place in bitter Arctic conditions. The 2,500 Japanese holding the island fought with the usual determination. By the time the Americans recaptured it, there were only 28 Japanese soldiers left alive. In August, 29,000 US Marines and 5,200 Canadians attacked the nearby island of Kiska. The assault was preceded by a heavy bombardment by bombers and battleships. The invaders met no resistance. What they didn't know was that the 6,000 Japanese troops defending the island had left weeks earlier.

ENTERTAINING THE TROOPS

Every general knows that the mood of his troops - their morale - is as important as their equipment and fighting skills. Civilians at home also need to feel they are on the winning side, and are contributing to victory. In the Second World War, both sides made great efforts to entertain their citizens, to keep their spirits up.

Star turns

On the Allied side, the war made lasting stars out of singers such as Vera Lynn and Dinah Shore, comedians Bob Hope and George Formby, and band leaders Glenn Miller and Tommy Dorsey. Already famous, they became associated forever with the intense and unforgettable war years. To us today, because of changing musical fashions, and overuse in TV documentaries, popular songs from the war often sound trite and sentimental. But when Vera Lynn sang, *"We'll meet again... don't know where, don't know when,"* it pulled at the heartstrings of millions of people separated from friends and relatives, who they might easily never see again.

Sheet music for *"We'll meet again"* - a tune that was very popular with Allied soldiers

INTERNET LINK

For a link to a website where you can listen to music from the Second World War, go to
www.usborne-quicklinks.com

Front line tours

Most of the big stars of the war were known mainly from their radio performances, although many also toured hospitals and factories and performed behind front lines. Some lesser known performers took greater risks and did shows much closer to the action, improvising as well as they could in fields, barns and bunkers.

The Soviet Union had over a thousand touring companies who entertained front line troops with sentimental ballads, dances, comedy routines and poetry readings. One Soviet entertainer recalls coming under German mortar attack during a show. On another occasion, the soldiers twice went off to fight, before returning to watch the rest of the show. American entertainment was provided by USO (United Services Organization); British by ENSA (Entertainments National Service Association) - although wits soon called it *Every Night Something Awful*.

Just behind the front line, a troupe of actors and musicians entertains Soviet soldiers, using a *T-34* tank as a makeshift stage.

Escape to Hollywood

Many films from the war years were propaganda pieces - created to record victories, or spur their audiences to greater efforts and sacrifices. Along with such action films as *In Which We Serve* and *Guadalcanal Diary*, were romances such as *Casablanca*, and comedies such as Charlie Chaplin's *The Great Dictator*.

Enemy radio

Enemy broadcasts were popular too - although in Germany and Japan those caught listening could face imprisonment or even execution. US soldiers in the Pacific listened to *Tokyo Rose* (American-born Iva Ikuko Toguri), whose flirtatious, silky voice was a siren call for men missing their sweethearts at home. British listeners tuned into the Nazi propaganda broadcasts of William Joyce, to laugh at his biased reporting of the war. His sneering, upper class voice earned him a nickname: *Lord Haw-Haw*.

SPECIAL FORCES

Some operations in the war were simply too dangerous or difficult to expect ordinary soldiers to carry them out. So special groups of highly-trained volunteers were used instead. Dropped behind enemy lines by boat, glider or parachute, these special forces stirred up havoc, before vanishing into the night.

Commandos

Formed after Dunkirk, British commando units swiftly became legendary. They were so effective that Hitler ordered any commando captured should be shot, rather than held prisoner. Commandos specialized in hit-and-run raids in occupied Europe. One raid in 1942, at St. Nazaire in France, destroyed a vast dry dock which was being used to repair German battleships. But of 611 commandos and sailors taking part, only 214 returned home. Another raid, in 1943, destroyed a German atomic weapons research laboratory in Norway.

The SAS (Special Air Service) was formed during the war, to assist British forces in North Africa. Its sabotage activities behind enemy lines were so successful that German soldiers were sent to kidnap the SAS leader, Lt. Col. David Stirling. They succeeded. Stirling spent the next two and a half years in prisoner-of-war camps. After escaping four times, he was sent to the infamous Colditz Castle in Germany. Field Marshal Montgomery described the young Stirling as, "quite mad, quite, quite mad. However in war there is often a place for mad people."

INTERNET LINK
For a link to a website where you can find an illustrated account of the mission to rescue Mussolini, go to **www.usborne-quicklinks.com**

American special forces, who were under the command of General Merrill, patrol the Burmese jungle in June 1944.

Long-term fighters

Most special forces operations rarely lasted more than a day, but some groups were formed to fight long-term campaigns. In Burma, occupying Japanese forces had to contend with two distinct guerrilla forces working way behind their front line. The Chindits, named after a mythical Burmese lion, were led by British Major General, Orde Wingate. The other unit - known as Merrill's Marauders - was commanded by US Brigadier General Frank D. Merrill. These groups struck at supply columns and bases and seriously undermined the Japanese army in Burma.

Scarface Skorzeny

Otto "Scarface" Skorzeny

One of the boldest raids of the war was when German commandos snatched Mussolini from a ski resort hotel in the Italian Abruzzi Mountains, where he was being held prisoner. They used gliders to land silently, right next to the hotel, bursting in on Mussolini and his captors, without having to fire a shot. The ex-dictator was quickly bundled into a small aircraft and flown to Hitler's headquarters. Leading the attack was SS Captain Otto Skorzeny, who was nicknamed "Scarface" because of a duelling injury.

In October 1944, Hitler feared his ally Hungary was about to surrender to the approaching Soviet army. He ordered Skorzeny, and a special unit of SS troops, to kidnap the son of the Hungarian leader, Admiral Horthy. Horthy had told his people their country was no longer at war, but this announcement was swiftly contradicted. Perhaps Skorzeny's greatest coup was when he used captured US vehicles and uniforms to disguise German troops in the Ardennes in December 1944. They destroyed supply dumps, and ambushed unsuspecting US units, causing widespread panic and confusion.

Mussolini, during his rescue by Skorzeny's glider troops

THE ITALIAN CAMPAIGN

In February 1945, as his world collapsed around him, Adolf Hitler complained, "It is quite obvious that our Italian alliance has been of more service to our enemies than to ourselves." Most Italians hadn't wanted their country to be involved in the war in the first place. As defeat loomed, the Italian government rose up against their leader Mussolini, and made peace with the Allies.

This map of Italy shows important cities and battles during the fighting that took place between 1943 and 1945.

The first steps into Italy

The Allied victory in North Africa in the spring of 1943 offered the Allies the chance to invade Italy from the south. On July 10, British, Canadian and American troops landed in Sicily. Within five weeks the island was theirs, and preparations were made to invade Italy itself. For the Italian government, the writing was on the wall. Mussolini was deposed and imprisoned, and secret surrender negotiations began with the Allies. This was a tricky business, as Italy was full of German troops. A surrender agreement was signed on September 3, 1943, the same day British troops crossed the Strait of Messina to the Italian mainland.

Six days later, the US army landed further north, at Salerno. For Germany, the Italian surrender made little difference. German soldiers simply disarmed the Italians and changed from being allies to behaving like an occupying force. Where possible, Italian soldiers changed sides. Within a few months, 350,000 of them were fighting with the Allies - rather than against them.

American artillery men advance through the dusty roads of Sicily, in September 1943.

Slow progress

Italy is a narrow, mountainous country, with many rivers crossing its interior. This made it easy to defend and difficult to attack. After early Allied success in the south, the Germans established a solid defensive line about 100km (60 miles) south of Rome. So Allied commanders decided to launch attacks along the coast instead. But the landing craft needed for such assaults were in short supply. The campaign to drive Japan from its Pacific empire was in full swing, and equipment in England was being stockpiled for the coming invasion of France. Allied soldiers landed at Anzio on January 22, 1944, but were hemmed in by strong German forces.

However, a few months later, two decisive victories finally enabled them to break through the German defensive ring and push further north. A group of mainly Polish forces overran a German strongpoint in the ancient hilltop monastery of Monte Cassino - destroying the 1,500-year-old historic site in the process. Within three weeks, the undefended Italian capital of Rome was in Allied hands. On June 6, the Allies landed at Normandy in France, and the war in Italy became something of a sideshow. But, by the end of the war, Allied forces in Italy had reached the River Po, and only the far north of the country remained in German hands.

INTERNET LINK
For a link to a website where you can watch a slide show of photographs taken during the Allied invasion of Sicily, go to
www.usborne-quicklinks.com

A grisly fate

Hitler had many appalling traits, but he could be very loyal to his friends. This included the imprisoned Mussolini, who he had rescued by German commandos. The Italian dictator, now a shadow of his former self, set up a new government in German-occupied Italy. It was called the Salo Republic, after the small northern town he made his headquarters. But Mussolini was now just a puppet - completely under Nazi control. In April 1945, he and his mistress, Clara Petacci, were captured and swiftly executed by Italian partisans. Their bodies were hung in a city square in Milan, to be spat and shot at by vengeful Italians.

WAR IN THE PACIFIC

The Allied campaign to clear the Pacific of Japanese forces gained an unstoppable momentum in 1944. But Japan was not yet a spent force. While many of its island fortresses were isolated and starved into submission, those that were attacked fought almost to the last man. And Japan's navy was still among the most powerful in the world.

The battle for the Philippines

In May 1944, US forces invaded Biak - an island north of New Guinea, and a vital stepping stone for their planned reconquest of the Philippines - and went on to take the Marianas Island chain. The Japanese counterattacked by sending a large fleet under Admiral Ozawa Jisaburo to repel the invaders. Ozawa's force contained four of Japan's largest aircraft carriers, and 326 planes took off to attack Admiral Marc A. Mitscher's US fleet. They were heading for disaster.

A US Marine searches for Japanese soldiers in the rubble of a destroyed defensive position on Saipan Island, June 1944.

The Turkey Shoot

On June 19, American pilots shot down 219 of these Japanese planes near the Marianas Islands, losing only 30 of their own. Planes fell out of the sky, like birds shot down by hunters, in an air battle that became known as the Marianas Turkey Shoot.

That same day, US submarines sank two Japanese aircraft carriers - and, the following day, US dive bombers sank a third. By the end of the battle, Admiral Ozawa had only 35 planes left. The impressive Japanese carrier force that had struck such a stunning blow at Pearl Harbor had been all but destroyed.

Vital islands

By August 10, American forces had cleared the islands of Saipan, Tinian and Guam, in the Marianas. The fighting had been hard. At Saipan, 32,000 Japanese troops had fought to the death. Another 22,000 Japanese civilians stationed on the island committed suicide.

The loss for Japan was extremely serious. American control of the islands gave them airbases from which their *B-29 Superfortress* bombers could attack Japan's major cities - only 2,000km (1,300 miles) to the north.

A last gamble

In October 1944, a vast US invasion fleet of 700 ships and 200,000 troops stormed towards Leyte in the Philippines, ready to tackle the Japanese garrison of 70,000 troops. In a final, desperate attempt to counteract this threat and repel the invasion, the Japanese navy mustered what was left of its forces. The two sides met at the Battle of Leyte Gulf. The battle posed a terrible risk for the Japanese. If they lost, their oil supplies in the East Indies would be cut off to them, and their naval power would be destroyed.

A Japanese *kamikaze* plane, set ablaze by anti-aircraft fire, narrowly misses a US aircraft carrier, sailing close to Saipan Island.

From October 23-25, the United States and Japan fought the greatest sea battle in history - over a vast area of the Pacific Ocean about the size of France. Although it was touch and go at times, the Americans eventually outflanked the Japanese. Japan lost 26 ships, including *Musashi*, one of the world's biggest battleships, and the United States lost seven ships.

The suicide pilots

The stakes at Leyte Gulf had been so high that the Japanese navy's defeat virtually guaranteed that Japan would lose the war. But Japan was not going to surrender easily. During the battle, American sailors were horrified to see that Japanese pilots had deliberately begun to crash their planes into American ships.

A *kamikaze* pilot wraps the Japanese flag around his head, as he prepares for his one-way mission.

This dramatic, last-ditch use of suicide pilots, who the Japanese named *kamikaze* (meaning "divine wind"), had never been seen before. But, over the following year, 1,228 Japanese airmen - mostly young and inexperienced - would deliberately sacrifice themselves in this way. And it was effective too. Altogether the *kamikaze* pilots managed to sink 34 American ships - and damage a further 288.

INTERNET LINK
For a link to a website where you can listen to US radio broadcasts reporting the progress of war in the Pacific, go to **www.usborne-quicklinks.com**

June 1944 to May 1945

THE DEFEAT OF GERMANY

British troops arrive on Sword Beach, during the Normandy Landings of June 6,
1944. It is 8:45 in the morning, and they are still under enemy fire, as they mill
around in the chaos of the opening hours of the invasion of Western Europe.

PREPARING FOR D-DAY

From 1941 until June 1944, most of the fighting took place in the Soviet Union and the Pacific. But, in England, the Allies had spent two years building up a powerful force, to invade and liberate Western Europe from the Nazis. People joked that the only thing stopping the island from sinking under the weight of all the men and equipment were the anti-aircraft barrage balloons that flew over every military base.

Commander-in-chief, General Eisenhower, visits parachute troops on the eve of the invasion. Within hours, these men were fighting and dying in France.

Expecting visitors

The Germans knew an invasion was inevitable - they had been expecting it for some time. From Norway to Spain, they had built concrete fortresses and heavy gun positions, and sewn the beaches with barbed wire, mines and anti-tank obstacles.

The Atlantic Wall, as it was known, looked formidable - but it had weaknesses. It was too long to defend strongly at any single point, and it was mostly held by second-rate soldiers. But there were still strong German forces in France, who would hurry at once to stop any invasion.

Where to start?

American general Dwight D. Eisenhower was given the enormous task of directing the invasion, of Canadian, British and American troops, codenamed *Operation Overlord*. He would have to break the Atlantic Wall, allow his men to land, then transport troops, tanks and other equipment - at great speed - before the Germans could throw them back into the sea. He also had to decide on a landing point. Calais was nearest, but it was strongly defended, and right in the north of France. Normandy, though further, offered a more direct way into the rest of France, and the entire south coast of England could be used as a launch point.

Getting ashore

British general Bernard Montgomery planned to land at five points along a 100km (60 mile) stretch of coast. Troops would arrive by sea in landing craft; others by parachute or glider. Once they captured a beachhead, they had to be able to land further troops and supplies at great speed. The ports were too well defended to attack, so the Allies had to make their own landing jetties. Two huge ones, codenamed *Mulberries*, were built from concrete sections, to be towed across the channel. PLUTO (a vast Pipe Line Under The Ocean) was laid down to provide fuel for vehicles.

Special weapons

Special weapons were developed to help the Allies in those first crucial hours. *Sherman* tanks were fitted with propellers and canvas "floatation collars" - to allow them to float ashore. Other tanks had rotating flails of steel chains attached to their fronts, to destroy mines buried on the beaches. Some tanks carried giant spools of fabric to be unravelled on soft sand, to allow other vehicles to get off the beach without sinking. But most fearsome of all were *Churchill* tanks fitted with napalm flame throwers. These could shoot a jet of fire 110m (360ft) towards enemy positions.

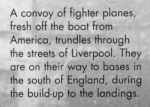

A convoy of fighter planes, fresh off the boat from America, trundles through the streets of Liverpool. They are on their way to bases in the south of England, during the build-up to the landings.

Faking it

Finally, the Allies pulled off an amazing confidence trick. Fake fuel and equipment dumps, as well as landing craft and airfields, were built in Kent - just across the Channel from Calais - to fool German reconnaissance aircraft and make the Germans think the invasion was really heading there instead. Radio signals for a non-existent new invasion army, based in Kent, buzzed across the airwaves. Even a small invasion fleet was assembled. When everything was ready, Eisenhower and his staff - and hundreds of thousands of soldiers, sailors and airmen - had to wait for the crucial moment to proceed.

INTERNET LINK

For a link to a website where you can find out about the machines invented for D-Day and follow an animated map of the landings, go to
www.usborne-quicklinks.com

THE D-DAY LANDINGS

The timing of the Normandy Landings was crucial. Tides, weather, moonlight - all had to be right. By early June, everything was ready, but unseasonable storms lashed the Channel. Then, forecasters predicted a lull on the night of June 5-6. Eisenhower, his troops already packed into invasion ships and barges, could wait no longer.

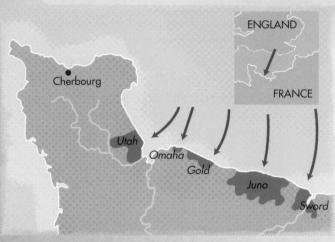

The arrows on this map show the direction of assault on the first day of the Landings. Each beachhead had its own codename, shown here.

From sky and sea

On June 5, a fleet of 5,000 ships moved out from the ports of southern England to assemble off the Normandy coast. That night, troops crowded into gliders and planes, and ground crews armed the fighters and bombers that accompanied the invasion force. In all, 9,000 aircraft took part. French Resistance forces were tipped off, via a coded message. Throughout France, railway lines and telephone exchanges were blown up - to hamper German forces heading for the coast. The invasion began at 12:16am on June 6 - known as D-Day - when three British gliders packed with troops landed just outside Caen, on the edge of the invasion zone. Their task was to capture vital roads and bridges or destroy enemy strongpoints.

Beach landings

For many soldiers in the landing crafts, the invasion began in a blur of seasickness, freezing spray, and noise from the guns of Allied warships and thousands of planes flying low overhead. By preventing attacks on the invaders, the planes were crucial to success. At 6:30am, the first seaborne troops landed at the poorly defended *Utah* beach. By nightfall 23,000 US troops had come ashore with only 200 casualties. *Omaha* beach would be much more difficult. Right from the start, landing craft were subjected to heavy artillery and machine-gun fire.

Mixed fortunes

Around 1,000 Americans were killed at *Omaha* beach; it was to be the worst bloodshed that day. British and Canadian troops landing further east had mixed fortunes. The beach landings were easier, but they met heavy German opposition as they tried to move inland. By the evening, 150,000 Allied troops had landed in Normandy. Casualties had been relatively light - only 2,500 men in total were killed.

American war photographer Robert Capa took this close-up of *Omaha* beach, in a series of photographs that made him famous.

INTERNET LINK

For a link to a website where you can read eyewitness accounts and newspaper clippings from the D-Day landings, go to **www.usborne-quicklinks.com**

Wrong again

Hitler was told of the Allied landings when he woke around midday. He was delighted. "As long as they were in Britain we couldn't get at them. Now we have them where we can destroy them." But his commanders on the ground were divided on what to do. Field Marshal von Rundstedt, commander-in-chief of all Germany's western forces, wanted to let the Allies build up their forces before he attacked in strength. This, he hoped, would allow him to destroy more of his enemy's troops. His second-in-command, Erwin Rommel, wanted an early attack, to destroy the Allies on their beachheads.

The die is cast

But the Germans were still convinced that the main attack would come at Calais, so they held back reinforcements. The Allies also completely dominated the skies, annihilating German troops and tanks as they headed up to Normandy. By the end of June, Eisenhower had 850,000 men and 150,000 vehicles ashore. His gamble had paid off. There was no doubt now that Germany would lose the war. The only question was how much longer it would take.

The very first troops to land on *Omaha* beach are already pinned down by murderous machine-gun fire from the high cliffs beyond the beach.

HITLER - THE MILITARY COMMANDER

Judged solely in terms of his impact on the world, Hitler was one of the most impressive military commanders in history. Nazi propaganda portrayed him as a military genius, and early German successes demonstrated his ability. But self-delusion was one of his greatest defects and as a commander he was deeply flawed. The German people paid a terrible price for his blunders.

Hitler in 1941, surrounded by his generals. His early successes made it difficult for his commanders to argue against him.

A flawed force

The Nazis spent the 1930s building a military force that was probably the most effective in the world. Their troops were brainwashed in Nazi ideology, and they had exceptional weapons which they used with great skill.

But, right from the start, Hitler deeply disliked and distrusted many of his generals. He thought them cautious and narrow-minded, while they felt he was reckless, and resented his interference with their battle plans.

For example, Hitler followed the battle for Stalingrad with a street map spread out before him, issuing orders from a distance concerning the day-to-day running of the battle. His decisions that soldiers should stand firm, when battlefield commanders wanted to retreat, lost the German army hundreds of thousands of men, as well as valuable equipment.

General Heinz Guderian wrote this damning epitaph: *"He had a special picture of the world, and every fact had to be fitted into that ... world. As he believed, so the world must be; but in fact it was a picture of another world."*

Hitler visits the Polish front, during the opening stages of the war. As the war turned against him, such visits became increasingly rare.

Bad planning

Military equipment was often in short supply. But Hitler was so sure of victory in the Soviet Union in 1941 that he ordered the production of weapons and ammunition for the army to be drastically reduced. Instead he switched resources to the air force and the navy, to defeat the British. Army weapons production resumed in 1942, but equipment did not reach troops until late summer.

Strategic errors

Hitler's greatest blunders were on a much larger scale, though. His decision to risk war with Britain and her empire was taken with no real thought of how such a substantial enemy was to be defeated. He fatally underestimated the strength of the Soviet Union, and his invasion of that vast country was to become his undoing. In December 1941, just when it became clear that the war there was going badly wrong, he declared war on the United States: the world's most powerful nation. Germany may have had the world's best army, but it had to fight the three strongest powers on earth.

Hitler's twisted ideology also placed huge demands on Germany's military strength. In 1943 and 1944, massive efforts were put into the transportation of millions of Jews to death camps, deploying trains, soldiers and other resources that could have been effectively used to help his beleaguered armies.

The July assassination plot

Whether it was because most Germans were in thrall to Hitler's vision of world domination, or because the *Gestapo* (the Secret Police) was so effective, there was little resistance to the Nazis inside Germany. Some generals had long despised the ex-corporal who treated them with such contempt, but it was only in 1944 that a serious plot was hatched to kill Hitler.

Led by glamorous war hero Colonel Claus von Stauffenberg, the plotters intended to kill him with a briefcase bomb planted in his headquarters. Then they planned to seize control of the country with the Home Army - units of the German army stationed in Germany. The bomb blew Hitler's trousers to tatters, but it failed to kill him. In the wake of the assassination attempt, 7,000 people were arrested, and between two and three thousand of them were executed.

Hitler (middle) with von Stauffenberg (far left), in Rastenburg, East Prussia, on July 15, 1944. Stauffenberg is carrying a bomb to kill Hitler. But, on this occasion, he was not able to set it off.

INTERNET LINK
For a link to a website with an account of the 1944 assassination attempt on Hitler, go to **www.usborne-quicklinks.com**

93

FIGHTING FOR FRANCE

Despite their huge numbers, it took the Allies over six weeks to break out from their Normandy beachheads. But, when they did, the German army that had fought so fiercely to hold back the invaders, crumbled before them. Ahead lay the French capital, Paris.

A French Resistance fighter, identifiable by his armband, joins Allied troops in street fighting on the way to Paris.

Fighting for France

The fighting in Normandy had been tough. High hedges and narrow roads made defending easy for the Germans. Thousands of dead cows, killed in artillery and aerial bombardment, lay all around, adding to the chaos and stench of death. But, by July 24, US troops under General Omar Bradley broke out south of Saint-Lo. By August the Germans were in full retreat, and a further Allied invasion from the Mediterranean added to their problems. Allied troops finally met up in central France in mid-September.

"Paris must be destroyed!"

Major General Dietrich von Choltitz had been given the unenviable task of defending Paris. In early August, Hitler had summoned him and ordered that if the German army had to abandon the city, "it must be utterly destroyed … nothing must be left standing, no church, no artistic monument." With this in mind, German engineers placed demolition charges in major buildings, and prepared to destroy Paris.

Second thoughts

Von Choltitz was a loyal, even ruthless general, who had served the Nazis well. But he found his orders too much to stomach. By a window high up in his Parisian headquarters, he spent a wistful evening staring out on this beautiful city. Below, a woman in a bright red dress cycled by. "I like these pretty Parisians," he told an aide. "It would be a tragedy to have to kill them and destroy their city."

Twists and turns

As the Allies drew closer to Paris, Eisenhower decided to bypass it. He did not want his troops to have to fight in the city, and ruin its historic buildings. Inside the capital, events were acquiring their own momentum. The police went on strike, and French Resistance groups rose up to confront their German occupiers. Barricades were set up in the streets, and sporadic fighting broke out. Fearing a bloodbath, Eisenhower changed his mind, and US and Free French forces headed for the city. Meanwhile, von Choltitz, at great risk to his own life, sent out a message to the approaching troops, telling them he was willing to surrender.

The Allies enter Paris

On August 25, 1944, Allied troops poured into the city. Some were greeted by cheering Parisians, who showered them with flowers and kisses. Others met sporadic but determined German resistance. Von Choltitz officially surrendered at 2:30pm. But, as the streets filled with cheering crowds, German snipers fired on them from the rooftops. It would be another 24 hours before they were flushed out from their hiding places.

On to Germany

The Allies continued their advance into the early autumn. The Belgian cities of Brussels and Antwerp fell on September 3, and the first American patrols crossed into Germany on September 11. But then the Allies came up against three significant obstacles: two great rivers - the Meuse and the Rhine - and a formidable line of concrete bunkers and antitank barriers, known as the West Wall. It was a good place to stop. After such a rapid advance, forward units were running short of supplies. For the moment, the war in the West came to a halt.

German officers, who have surrendered during the liberation of Paris, eye their captors warily.

INTERNET LINK

For a link to a website where you can listen to the sound of Parisians celebrating the German surrender, and read eyewitness accounts, go to **www.usborne-quicklinks.com**

Crowds who took to the streets to celebrate the liberation of Paris are fired on by German snipers.

MOTHER OF INVENTION

Creativity has always blossomed in wartime. The development of new weapons and tactics can give one side a crucial advantage over the other. During the Second World War, scientists worked around the clock to produce extraordinary new weapons, machines and medicines - all in a fraction of the time it would have taken to produce them in peacetime.

The first jet planes

A British engineer named Frank Whittle invented a jet engine in 1930. But the British government wasn't interested in his idea at the time. It was the Germans, operating completely independently, who first flew a plane powered by a jet rather than a propeller.

The Germans went on to design the highly effective *Messerschmitt Me-262*, the first jet fighter to be used in combat and the most sophisticated fighter plane of the war. At 870kmph (540mph), it flew considerably faster than Allied planes. The *Me-262* was the most deadly adversary for American bombers. But, fortunately for the Allies, it wasn't introduced until 1944 and only a few were ever built. If they had been produced in greater numbers, it might have changed the course of the war. But Hitler insisted the new jet should be fitted with bombs and used to support ground troops. It was only used as a fighter plane when this proved to be a failure.

Two British scientists at work on the mass production of life-saving penicillin

Magic medicine

Since the late 19th century, scientists had known that some fungi could destroy bacteria which cause infections. But they weren't able to put this knowledge to use. In 1929, Alexander Fleming extracted a substance from the fungus *penicillium* which he named penicillin. Tests showed penicillin could be used to fight infections. Ten years later, Australian Howard Florry and German refugee Ernst Chain developed Fleming's work, and within a short time this new drug was being mass-produced in great vats, saving the lives of thousands of Allied soldiers.

The German jet-propelled
Messerschmitt Me-262

T-2-4012

Creating oil from coal

Military forces always need vast quantities of fuel, for their tanks, ships and planes, and for vehicles to transport their soldiers and artillery. The Germans had no fuel supplies of their own, and relied on the oil deposits of their ally Rumania. But this was never enough to supply all their needs. So, German scientists devised a technique to produce oil from a raw material Germany had a lot of: coal. This process, which involved mixing pulverized coal with high pressure hydrogen gas, was extremely effective. By 1944, 25 synthetic petroleum plants were producing at least half of all Germany's fuel.

Inventions that didn't work

As the war progressed, revolutionary new weapons were developed - from radio-guided missiles, to bouncing bombs designed to leapfrog over anti-torpedo nets. But not all these inventions worked. One, known as the *Panjandrum*, was designed to smash through concrete fortifications on the heavily defended coastline of France. It consisted of two enormous metal wheels, with two tons of explosives in its stubby axle. The wheels were driven by rocket engines placed all along the rim. It looked like a gigantic Catherine Wheel - and it was a disaster. Once unleashed, it was impossible to predict which way it would go!

This is a very rare photograph of the *Panjandrum*, during one of its farcical trials on an isolated British beach. On the outer rim of the wheel, you can make out the rocket engines that were supposed to drive it along.

INTERNET LINK

For a link to a website where you can find out more about some of the inventions and discoveries made during the war years, go to **www.usborne-quicklinks.com**

Simple ideas

Some of the best new ideas didn't rely on complicated machines at all. British bombers used a very simple and effective technique to confuse enemy radar about where a bomber attack was heading. They dropped reams of thin strips of tinfoil known as *Window*. These were picked up by German radar operators as a signal on their screens which looked like thousands of bombers.

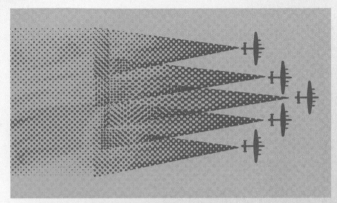

This diagram shows a small formation of British bombers dropping *Window* tin foil to confuse German radar operators.

SPECIAL RELATIONSHIPS

The two great partnerships of the war fought in very different ways. The Allies - principally the United States, the Soviet Union and Britain - cooperated closely. But the main Axis powers - Germany, Italy and Japan - made almost no effort to work together. This was to have a major effect on the outcome of the war.

Common bonds

The fact that Britain and the United States shared a language and democratic culture contributed greatly to their wartime cooperation. But they also worked well with their other principal ally - the totalitarian communist regime of Soviet Russia. When told of the Nazi invasion of the Soviet Union, the famously anti-communist Winston Churchill remarked: "If Hitler invaded Hell, I would at least make a favourable reference to the Devil…" All three countries recognized that - whatever their differences - nothing was more important than defeating the Nazis.

Churchill, Roosevelt and Stalin (left to right) meet to decide the fate of the world, in the Soviet town of Yalta, on the Black Sea in February 1945.

The Atlantic alliance

The United States and Britain had worked together even before Pearl Harbor, as President Roosevelt wanted to help in the war, without involving American troops. In the Lend-Lease Act of 1941, the US government put aside seven billion dollars to supply weapons and equipment to Britain. When the Axis powers declared war on the United States, Churchill and Roosevelt met up at once to forge a common strategy. They decided Germany should be defeated first, and then Japan. US and British forces fought together effectively in the Mediterranean and Europe. Their efforts were coordinated by a group of top military men, known as the Combined Chiefs of Staff, all under a single commander-in-chief. The Americans conducted their own campaign in the Pacific, where the British played a smaller part.

Close collaboration was not as necessary with Soviet forces, as they were fighting in different parts of the world. Nonetheless, the United States and Britain sent millions of dollars' worth of military equipment, food and supplies, to help the Soviets.

Vital meetings

The three Allied leaders, Roosevelt, Churchill and Stalin, met during the war - to ensure they worked well together, and to agree what would happen at the end of the war. At Teheran, in 1943, they discussed the invasion of Western Europe. At Yalta, in 1945, Stalin promised the Soviet Union would help the United States to defeat Japan. The three leaders also accepted that, after the war, Eastern Europe would be ruled by regimes loyal to the Soviets, but Western Europe and the Mediterranean would be left under the control of democratic governments.

This American poster celebrates the Allied war effort. Among other flags you can see those of the United States, Britain, the Soviet Union, China and Australia.

An Italian propaganda poster celebrating the Japanese attack on Pearl Harbor

The other side

By contrast, the Axis powers barely worked together at all, even when they were fighting on the same battlegrounds. Most German soldiers despised their Axis comrades, as they felt they fought badly. But the truth was that most of them had been sent to fight a war they had no desire to be in. Italian and German cooperation with the Japanese was almost non-existent. The Japanese didn't even forewarn them of the Pearl Harbor attack, and Japan didn't declare war on Germany's greatest enemy, the Soviet Union. Throughout the war, American ships flying the Soviet flag sailed to Russia's Pacific coast with weapons and supplies, and none were ever attacked by Japanese submarines.

INTERNET LINK
For a link to a website where you can watch archive film footage of a meeting between the three Allied leaders, go to **www.usborne-quicklinks.com**

GERMANY'S ILL-FATED CITIES

Throughout the war, people lived in fear of bombing - and with good reason. Cities such as London, Warsaw and Rotterdam were badly damaged by German bombers at the start of the war. As the war progressed, the Allies concentrated their huge industrial resources on building thousands of bombers and began attacking German cities with increasing intensity.

Cologne and Hamburg

On the night of May 30, 1942, for the first time in history, a stream of over a thousand bombers - 110 km (70 miles) long - took part in a single raid on the city of Cologne. Fewer than 500 people were killed, but 45,000 were made homeless. The Allies found that incendiary bombs could be made more effective if high explosive bombs were dropped first. This worked to chilling effect in Hamburg, on the night of July 24-25, 1943. Incendiary fires merged into one great conflagration. As hot air rose into the sky, cold air was sucked into the middle of the blazing city, creating a firestorm, which melted windows and set alight the asphalt streets. Tornado-like winds sucked cars and people into the flames. Even those seeking safety in bomb shelters suffocated for lack of oxygen.

The destruction of Dresden

The most infamous raid of the war was on the city of Dresden. Firestorms raged for a week, killing at least 35,000 people, mainly women and children, and destroying 25,000 of its 28,500 inner-city houses. (The casualty figure may even have been higher because the city was full of refugees fleeing from the advancing Russian army.) "We did not recognize our street anymore. Fire, only fire, wherever we looked," recalled a German child who survived, "there were burning vehicles and carts with refugees, people, horses, all of them screaming and shouting in fear of death." Even the zoo was destroyed. One keeper remembers having to shoot the big cats in case they escaped and went looking for people to eat.

Hamburg citizens wade through the ruins of their city, in July 1943. Hamburg was the first city to suffer destruction by firestorm.

Right or wrong?

The commander of British bomber forces, Air Marshal Arthur Harris, reported: "Dresden was a mass of munitions works, an intact government centre, and a key transportation point to the East. It is now none of these things." This was all true - yet the bombing of this historic and beautiful city remains one of the most controversial Allied actions of the entire war. Critics claim that the city had little military value, and that as many as 135,000 may have died. Some suggest raids like these constitute "war crimes" - just like the German massacres of civilians or the wholesale destruction of the Jews.

Those defending the raid support Harris's assertion that Dresden was a weapons manufacturing city, and an important rail link for German troops heading for the Eastern Front. But even British Prime Minister Winston Churchill was alarmed by the scale of the destruction. As the war drew to a close, he worried that, "we shall come into control of an utterly ruined land."

A stone figure on top of Dresden Town Hall looks down on the devastated city, after the firestorm of February 13-14, 1945.

TO GERMANY'S EASTERN BORDER

After Kursk there was only one possible conclusion to the war in the East. Although the German army was a superbly trained and organized fighting force, it couldn't match the sheer weight of Soviet forces pitted against it. 1944 was to become known as "the year of ten victories" in the Soviet Union.

A scorched earth retreat

The Germans conducted a "scorched earth" retreat through territory they had marched through so confidently two or three years before. Their arrogance and brutality had stirred up a vengeful force against them. Now they felt, said one soldier, "like a man who has seized a wolf by the ears, and dare not let go." The Soviets advanced relentlessly, but they did so at a terrible cost. The Germans still fought very effectively. Wherever they clashed, the Red Army suffered far higher casualties. But they still had more men. By 1944, their army numbered six million, with another million in reserve. The German forces amounted to a dwindling three and a half million.

INTERNET LINK
For a link to a website where you can find film footage, eyewitness accounts and more from the Warsaw Uprising, go to **www.usborne-quicklinks.com**

The Soviets fight back

On June 22, 1944, three years to the day after the Nazi invasion, four Soviet armies launched a massive assault against German Army Group Centre. Outnumbered ten to one, and with strict orders from Hitler not to surrender, the Germans were wiped out. By late July Soviet troops were a mere 13km (eight miles) from the Polish capital, Warsaw. Moscow Radio was urging the Poles to rise up and help them in the liberation of the city.

A Polish rebellion

Inside the heavily defended capital, 40,000 men of the Polish underground rose up in rebellion. Under the command of General Tadeusz Komorowski, they formed part of the Home Army. In four days, they seized three-fifths of the city, but disaster quickly overtook them. The Germans struck hard against the approaching Soviet forces, driving many of them back 100km (60 miles). German reinforcements poured into Warsaw, intent on destroying the Polish rebels. Brutal house-to-house fighting followed; over 200,000 civilians were killed. By the end of August, Poles were hiding in cellars, parched and starved, many weak from dysentery. Still, men, women, and even children, continued to fight against the Germans with great determination.

From bad to worse

Many of the German forces were desperate men too - with little to lose. They included soldiers from punishment battalions, and Russian deserters who had been persuaded to fight against their own country. These men behaved with merciless barbarity towards anyone they captured. Gradually, the Polish resistance was limited to the northern district of Warsaw. As their strength ebbed away, their only hope was that the Red Army would arrive to capture the city. But although Churchill and Roosevelt had asked Stalin for help, this never came.

Some historians believe Stalin deliberately denied them help - because the Home Army was loyal to the Polish government in exile in London, and he didn't want them to return to rule Poland. The Soviets claimed, with good reason, that they themselves were running short of supplies and faced tough opposition outside the city. But, surprisingly, given the ruthless way the Nazis usually dealt with rebellions, the Home Army managed to negotiate a surrender. On October 3, 15,000 of them marched off to prisoner-of-war camps.

Crouching behind the grand pillars of the Warsaw Opera House, German soldiers come under attack from the Polish Home Army.

INTO GERMANY FROM THE WEST

As 1944 drew to a close, American, British and Canadian forces stood ready to pour into Germany. But they were overstretched, exhausted and poorly coordinated. An autumn offensive at Arnhem, intending to open the way to Berlin, failed. In December, the German army counterattacked in force, causing US general George Patton to observe, "We can still lose this war."

Seizing bridges

Following the great victories in France and Belgium, British Field Marshal Montgomery suggested a bold strategy to reach Berlin quickly. Allied forces would seize important bridges in the Netherlands, then press through north Germany to Berlin.

General Eisenhower, the Allied Supreme Commander, was against the idea. He preferred an advance across a broad front. But Montgomery was given the chance to put his plan into operation. It almost worked. Bridges at Eindhoven and Nijmegan were captured by parachute troops, but the most northerly bridge, Arnhem, could not be held. Of 10,000 British paratroops dropped to seize the bridge, barely 2,000 managed to escape back to Allied lines.

A German tank passes columns of US prisoners during the Battle of the Bulge, December 17, 1944.

The Battle of the Bulge

Seriously weakened by five years of war, the German army was still a formidable fighting force. As the Allies closed in, the Germans fought back with even greater ferocity. On December 16, a sudden, unexpected German counterattack began. New tanks, kept for such an offensive, lurched through fog and snow in the thick forest of the Ardennes in Belgium.

A great bulge developed in the Allied line, as US troops retreated in confusion. Panic spread when it was discovered that the Germans were using special commando units dressed in US army uniforms. But December 23 brought clear blue skies, perfect for the Allies' great strength: their air power. German tanks and troops were mercilessly battered by planes carrying rockets and bombs, and the advance ground to a halt. The battle had been Hitler's last chance to turn the tide of the war, and it had failed. In early 1945, the Allies moved into Germany in force.

INTERNET LINK
For links to websites where you can find photographs, maps and eyewitness acounts of the Battle of the Bulge, go to
www.usborne-quicklinks.com

Germany in chaos

The Allies were hampered by two major obstacles: the Ruhr area had been deliberately flooded, and the great Rhine river blocked the way east. But in March they crossed the river and were advancing swiftly, sometimes covering 80km (50 miles) a day. In April, German forces in the Ruhr were encircled and 400,000 were taken prisoner - the greatest capitulation of the war in the West so far.

Germany was in chaos. Soviet troops had invaded, and millions were fleeing from them in terror. Squads of fanatical Nazis were executing any soldier who dared suggest surrender. Hitler, directing what was left of his forces from a bunker in Berlin, grew increasingly out of touch with reality. Before the war, he had said, "We may be destroyed, but if we are, we shall drag the world with us ... a world in flames." He intended to keep his word.

Orders were given to destroy everything in the Allies' path: bridges, power stations, hospitals. "If the war is lost, the German nation will also perish," Hitler told his minister Albert Speer. "There is no need to take into consideration the basic needs of the people. Those that remain after the battle are those who are inferior; for the good will have fallen."

THE FALL OF BERLIN

In the last weeks of the war, farce mixed with tragedy. Hitler, directing non-existent armies from his bunker in central Berlin, grew increasingly shrill and deranged. Stalin was determined to take Berlin - whatever the cost. And millions of soldiers - on all sides - wondered if, having got this far, they would be the ones to die in this last great battle.

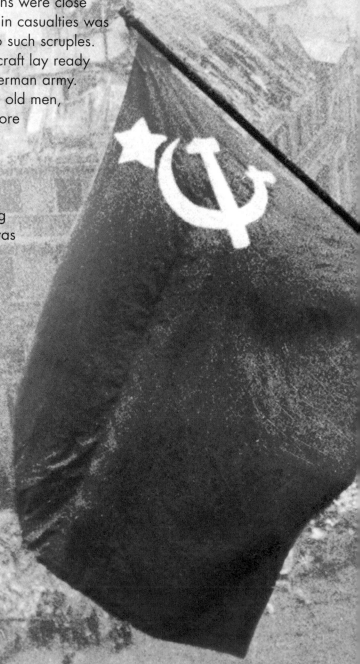

As smoke rises over the rubble-strewn streets of Berlin, a Russian soldier flies the Soviet flag from the roof of the German parliament, right in the middle of the city.

No escape

Throughout late 1944, Soviet forces had been pressing west through Eastern Europe. By February 1945, they were waiting on the River Oder, just outside Berlin, building up their strength for an assault. The Americans were close too, but Eisenhower had already decided the expected cost in casualties was not worth the prestige of capturing the capital. Stalin had no such scruples. 2,500,000 men, 6,000 tanks, 41,000 guns and 7,500 aircraft lay ready and waiting. Facing them was the tattered remains of the German army. Alongside these war-weary veterans were newly conscripted old men, and boys so young they could barely pick up a rifle, who wore helmets that were too big for their heads.

Panic in the streets

As the Soviets approached, millions of Germans fled, leaving behind a shattered capital. Already ruined by bombing, it was to be further destroyed by fearsome artillery barrages, and street-to-street fighting. An aura of unreality descended. Executed soldiers dangled from lampposts, hung for desertion to deter others from doing so. People staggered drunkenly through the chaos, trying to blot out the awful reality of what was about to happen. One possibly true story from this time tells that after a final performance of Wagner's *Götterdämmerung*, members of the audience filed past boys of the Hitler Youth who carried baskets of cyanide suicide capsules provided for them.

The battle for Berlin began on April 16. By April 24, the city was surrounded by Soviet troops. As they advanced into the suburbs, German army communication lines broke down completely. To find out how near the Russians were, officers in central command posts had to ring outlying districts via the city's public telephone network. When a voice answered the phone in Russian, they knew the end was a little nearer.

Wrong place, wrong time

During their invasion of the Soviet Union, the Nazis had behaved with great inhumanity towards both Soviet citizens and soldiers. For the Soviets entering Berlin ("the lair of the Fascist beast" - according to Soviet propaganda), the time for revenge was at hand. Unfortunately, those who suffered most were civilians. With over two million Soviet soldiers now in Berlin, thousands of women who had stayed on in the capital were raped.

The final act

Hitler spent the last few weeks in an underground bunker in central Berlin. In a feverish, hysterical atmosphere, he found time to marry his mistress, Eva Braun, and to denounce the German people in an unapologetic final political testament. They had, he said, shown themselves unworthy of the faith he had placed in them. Then, in the nearest he came to taking any of the blame for the disaster he had brought his country, this most ruthless and barbaric of leaders declared he had not been ruthless enough: "Afterwards, you regret the fact you have been so kind."

On April 30, 1945, Hitler took cyanide and shot himself in the head. Eva Braun killed herself too. Their bodies were burned, without ceremony, outside the bunker. A week later, on May 8, the war in Europe was over.

February to September 1945

THE DEFEAT OF JAPAN

In one of the most famous photographs of the war, US Marines plant the stars and stripes on top of Mount Suribachi, Iwo Jima, on February 23, 1945. The capture of this small island was hugely significant, as it was the first piece of Japanese home territory to fall into American hands.

IWO JIMA AND OKINAWA

As the war in Europe reached its inevitable conclusion, US forces in the Pacific began their final island battles before the invasion of Japan. In February and April, 1945, they invaded two formidably defended Japanese islands: Iwo Jima and Okinawa. The Japanese knew they couldn't hold the islands, but they hoped to inflict such dreadful casualties on the invaders that President Roosevelt would be forced to negotiate a compromise peace.

Iwo Jima

Barely 20 square km (8 square miles) in area, Iwo Jima was defended by 21,000 Japanese soldiers, who had been ordered to fight to the death. This was, after all, the first piece of Japanese home territory to be invaded in 4,000 years. The tiny island was an ugly slab of black volcanic rock and scrub. It had once been used as a fighter airbase, but had been turned into a formidable fortress of concrete gun emplacements and pillboxes, linked together by tunnels.

Approaching the island from Hawaii, trailing 110km (70 miles) along the ocean, was an invasion fleet of 800 vessels and 300,000 men. 100,000 of them were marine combat troops, and the invasion was set for February 19.

A US Marine dashes forward under a hail of machine-gun fire, during the battle for Okinawa, in May 1945.

Concentrated carnage

Shortly after the first American landing craft hit the island beaches, Japanese forces began a withering bombardment. For the next month, American soldiers and marines would have to struggle for every inch of the island. Because their Japanese opponents were so well hidden, the Americans usually didn't see them until they were dead. The fighting ended on March 16. Of the defenders, only 216 surrendered; the rest fought to the death. 6,000 Americans were killed; 17,000 wounded.

Worse to come

The next target to be invaded was an even tougher nut to crack. Okinawa, a narrow island, 110km (70 miles) long, was only 500km (300 miles) from mainland Japan. Most of the 100,000 Japanese troops there were dug into three strong defensive ridges in the south of the island. They peered out from a dense well-concealed network of caves and tunnels, and they too had been ordered to fight to the last man.

On Easter Day, April 1, 1945, another gigantic armada began to land 172,000 US troops on Okinawa. The fighting that followed was the bloodiest of the entire Pacific War. Torrential rain lashed the island, reducing the battlefield to a muddy quagmire. With its well dug-in defenders and endless mud, the fighting reminded some marine veterans of the trenches of the Western Front during the First World War.

INTERNET LINK
For a link to a website where you can watch archive film footage of the fighting on Iwo Jima, go to **www.usborne-quicklinks.com**

A nightmare campaign

Eventually, with flame-throwers and high explosives blasting the Japanese from their positions, the Americans captured the island. It took three months and cost them 5,500 dead and 51,000 wounded. Japanese casualties were far worse, although a surprising 11,000 surrendered. During the campaign, the US fleet had stayed offshore, to resupply their forces inland, and bombard Japanese positions. But the Japanese had sent 800 *kamikaze* planes to bomb them, with devastating effect: they sank 32 US ships and damaged 368. The Americans had paid a great price to win these two small islands. Now they faced the invasion of Japan itself.

Just behind the front lines, men of the 77th Infantry division in Okinawa listen to the news of Germany's surrender on May 8, 1945. A minute later, they were back at their posts, killing or being killed.

THE MANHATTAN PROJECT

In the 1930s, scientists working in nuclear physics realized they could use the energy inside atoms of uranium and plutonium to create an immense explosive. Over the next decade or so, Allied and Axis scientists carried out research aimed at constructing the world's first atomic bomb. What they all knew for certain was that any nation who possessed such a weapon would be able to win the war.

Robert Oppenheimer - the scientist in charge of the Manhattan Project. Like many of his colleagues, he was very uneasy about producing the A-Bomb.

Selling the idea

Fearing that Germany, or even Japan, might win the race to build a working atomic bomb, Allied scientists tried to persuade American politicians to fund the development of their own. But the science behind it was so bizarre, they were not taken seriously. There are, for example, 200 million volts of electricity in a single atom of uranium. The world's greatest living scientist, Albert Einstein, even wrote to President Roosevelt to try to interest him in the project. But Einstein got a cool response. "What would America want with such a weapon?" reasoned the President.

International team effort

But war with Japan and Germany changed the President's mind. Funding was made available, and a brilliant American physicist named Robert Oppenheimer put together an international research team to develop a working atomic bomb. The enterprise was codenamed the *Manhattan Project* and based in a warren of laboratories in Los Alamos, a remote spot in the New Mexican desert.

INTERNET LINK

For a link to a website where you can find out about the people involved in the Manhattan Project, go to
www.usborne-quicklinks.com

This extraordinary photo shows the awesome power of the first ever atomic bomb explosion. Within .062 of a second, when the shot was taken, the fireball is already over 300m (900 feet) wide.

The Los Alamos laboratory in New Mexico, where the world's first atomic bomb was created.

A lucky break

In an amazing twist of Allied good fortune, many of the world's top atomic scientists were political or Jewish refugees from Germany and Italy. Hitler had seriously underestimated them. "If the dismissal of Jewish scientists means the annihilation of contemporary German science, we shall have to do without science for a few years," he claimed. Without them, or the Americans' vast resources, the Axis had no chance of building a bomb. But the Allies didn't know this. Their research was driven by the fear that Germany would beat them to it.

Vast expense

Research continued with desperate haste. "Tickling the dragon" was the term scientists used to refer to their dangerous work. The Manhattan Project blossomed into a business as vast as the American motor industry, in its size and use of resources. It cost two billion dollars, and its factories and research laboratories were staffed by 600,000 people. Despite these vast sums and numbers, it remained a secret. Even the vice president, Harry Truman, didn't know about it until he became president, when Roosevelt died in April 1945.

The bombs

As explosives, uranium and plutonium are very powerful. An amount of either the size of a large orange is equivalent to 20,000 tons of TNT - the explosive most commonly used in Second World War shells and bombs. The bombs developed by the Manhattan Project worked like this:

Uranium bomb
A uranium projectile, shaped like this, is fired along a barrel into another quantity of uranium. On impact, there is a vast explosion.

Plutonium bomb
A ring of uranium projectiles, like this, are fired into a central core of plutonium, producing a similarly vast explosion.

A trial run

By the summer of 1945, the Manhattan Project scientists had produced two different atomic bombs. One, using the element uranium, they were sure would work. The other, using the man-made material plutonium, was more of an uncertainty. To test it, a tall tower was constructed at Alamogordo, in the New Mexican desert, and the bomb was placed on top. Successfully detonated on July 16, 1945, it sent a plume of radioactive smoke and sand 12,000m (40,000ft) into the sky. By this stage of the war, Japan was the only Axis power left fighting. US politicians were afraid that invading Japan would involve a terrible cost in American lives. The atomic bomb offered the opportunity to end the war - with one final, dramatic flourish.

Oppenheimer, together with an American general, stands at the exact point of detonation of the first atomic bomb. All that remains of the tower the bomb was placed on are a few twisted strands of metal, and the surrounding desert sand has been turned to glass.

HIROSHIMA & NAGASAKI

Throughout the summer of 1945, Japanese forces resisted their inevitable defeat with such ferocity that Allied planners feared the invasion of Japan itself would cost half a million lives. The atomic bomb presented an opportunity for the Allies to destroy their tenacious enemies in a single flash of terrible fire.

Where to go?

The Americans chose their targets carefully. They wanted to bomb a city that was an important military hub. They also wanted a target that had been relatively untouched by the bombing raids of the previous year, so they could see exactly how much damage their new weapon was capable of doing. This ruled out Tokyo, which had already been devastated by bombers in March, in a raid that had killed 100,000 and left fires burning for four days.

The city selected to be destroyed was Hiroshima, a military supply base with shipyards, weapons factories, and a population of 300,000. The pilot chosen for the mission was Col. Paul Tibbets, who would fly the *B-29 Superfortress Enola Gay* from Tinian airbase in the Marianas Islands. After being given the go-ahead, Tibbets and his crew were delayed by a whole five days, waiting for the weather to clear.

Beneath this fearsome mushroom cloud of radiated smoke and rubble lies the city of Hiroshima.

This aerial photograph of Hiroshima was taken a few days after the attack. The city has been almost entirely flattened by a single bomb.

A peep into hell

Enola Gay, and two other planes packed with scientific equipment, arrived over the clear blue sky of Hiroshima shortly after 8:00am on August 6. Their uranium bomb, codenamed *Little Boy*, exploded 576m (1,890ft) above the city. In the flash and blast that followed, factories, office blocks and homes were flattened. Commuters in trains were flung topsy-turvy into the air. Grass, flowers and trees in city parks burst into flames. People caught outdoors were vaporized. Only their shadows remained, caught in the superheated flash of the atomic detonation. Watching from above, "a peep into hell" was how *Enola Gay*'s tail gunner described the dreadful sight.

Horrifying destruction

About two-thirds of the city was destroyed in an instant - along with 80,000 of its citizens. Over the following months and years, another 80,000 died of radiation poisoning. The Japanese government was too stunned to react. Communications were totally destroyed between Hiroshima and Tokyo. When news of the annihilation eventually reached the Japanese capital, it was dismissed as an exaggeration.

Unlucky Nagasaki

On August 9, another *B-29*, *Bocks Car*, was dispatched from Tinian, carrying a plutonium type bomb, codenamed *Fat Man*. Their target was the great weapons arsenal of Kokura, but when they arrived it was covered by thick cloud. The city hovered on the brink of destruction - but the bomb aimer couldn't see his target. So the plane flew another hundred miles southwest, to the industrial city of Nagasaki, dropping the bomb over it at 11:00am. The damage wasn't as great as at Hiroshima - there was less to destroy - but just as many people died.

A double blow

The previous day, the Soviet Union had declared war on Japan, and invaded Manchuria. But still the Japanese government argued over surrender. Emperor Hirohito and most of his ministers wanted the fighting to stop. But this provoked a revolt among senior army officers, determined to fight to the end. Fortunately, the revolt failed. Fighting stopped on August 15, and a surrender was signed on September 2, 1945 - six years and a day after the war began.

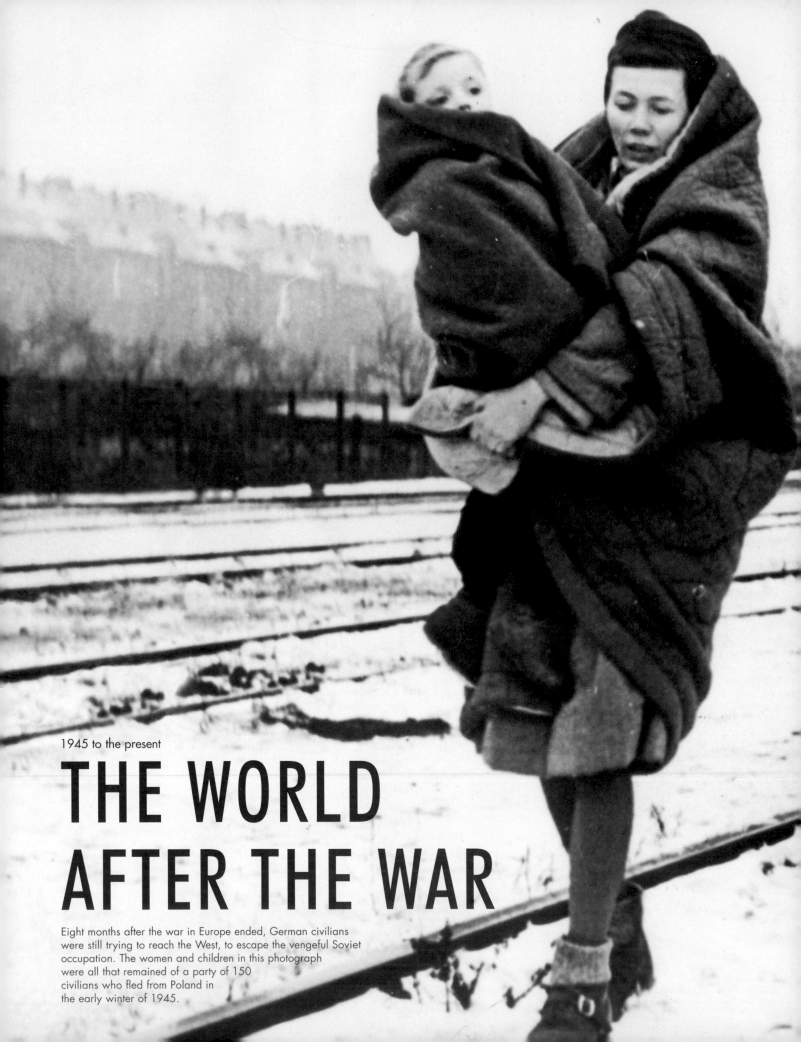

1945 to the present

THE WORLD
AFTER THE WAR

Eight months after the war in Europe ended, German civilians
were still trying to reach the West, to escape the vengeful Soviet
occupation. The women and children in this photograph
were all that remained of a party of 150
civilians who fled from Poland in
the early winter of 1945.

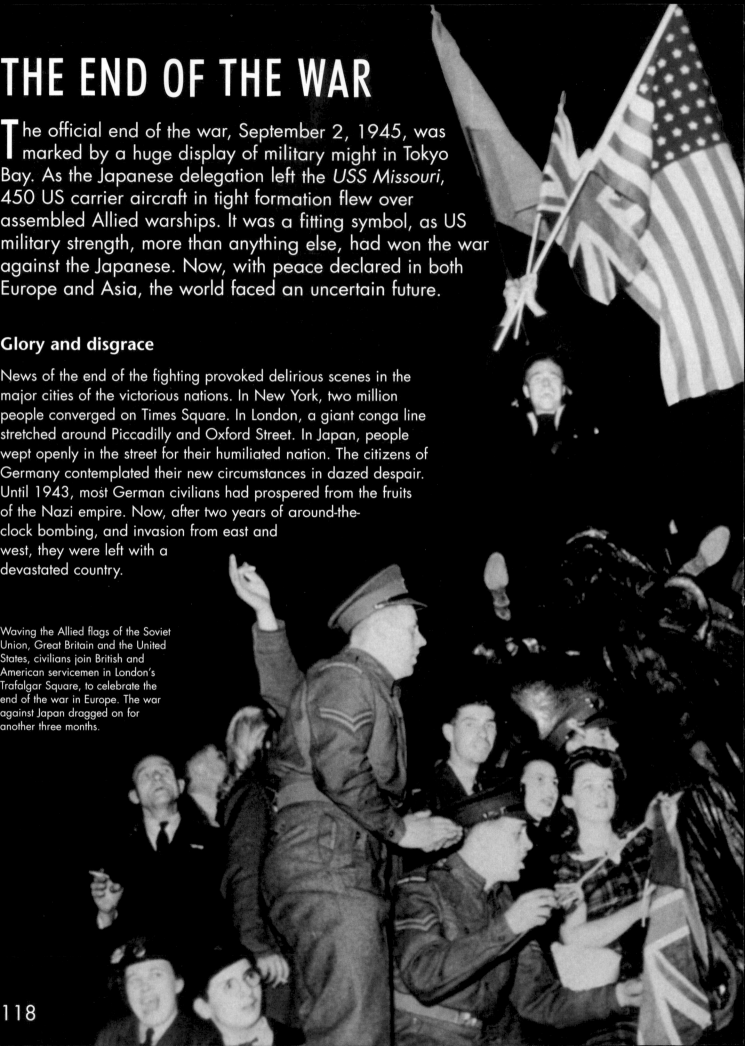

THE END OF THE WAR

The official end of the war, September 2, 1945, was marked by a huge display of military might in Tokyo Bay. As the Japanese delegation left the *USS Missouri*, 450 US carrier aircraft in tight formation flew over assembled Allied warships. It was a fitting symbol, as US military strength, more than anything else, had won the war against the Japanese. Now, with peace declared in both Europe and Asia, the world faced an uncertain future.

Glory and disgrace

News of the end of the fighting provoked delirious scenes in the major cities of the victorious nations. In New York, two million people converged on Times Square. In London, a giant conga line stretched around Piccadilly and Oxford Street. In Japan, people wept openly in the street for their humiliated nation. The citizens of Germany contemplated their new circumstances in dazed despair. Until 1943, most German civilians had prospered from the fruits of the Nazi empire. Now, after two years of around-the-clock bombing, and invasion from east and west, they were left with a devastated country.

Waving the Allied flags of the Soviet Union, Great Britain and the United States, civilians join British and American servicemen in London's Trafalgar Square, to celebrate the end of the war in Europe. The war against Japan dragged on for another three months.

Displaced persons

The most immediate problem was what to do with the millions of people the war had uprooted. In Germany, there were five and a half million Soviet citizens who needed to be sent home. Among them were soldiers who had fought for the Nazis and faced certain execution at home. But, with a cruel logic, the Soviet authorities decided that many of the others, who had survived captivity as prisoners-of-war and slave workers, were "traitors" too. So they returned home to long prison sentences. Millions of Germans had also fled west from the approaching Soviet armies in the East. In the months before and after the end of the war, as many as two million of these refugees may have died of starvation, disease and exhaustion.

Retribution

Representatives of the old regimes were rounded up. The Soviets shot any Nazi official from the rank of mayor and above, partly in reprisal for the Nazi practice of automatically executing any communist official they had captured in Soviet territory. In other European countries, those who had collaborated - cooperated with the German invaders - were punished too. In France, 120,000 collaborators were given prison sentences, and 2,000 were executed. Another 50,000 or so, who escaped "official" justice, were murdered in the years after the war.

Changing hearts and minds

In Japan and Germany, people loyal to their former regimes faced re-education. This process was awkwardly known as demilitarization - or *de-Nazification*. In Germany, for example, citizens were taken to see the victims of nearby concentration camps, or shown films of recently liberated death camps such as Auschwitz.

These German civilians have been taken on a tour of a concentration camp, to show them the true nature of the Nazi regime.

The terrible price of war

With the fighting over, it was now possible to begin to estimate the human cost. Most historians accept the war claimed at least 50 million lives. The Soviet Union suffered the worst, with over 25 million military and civilian deaths. Shockingly, only 3% of Soviet men aged between 19 and 23 survived. German dead numbered three and a half million military men, and over two million civilians. Britain and her Commonwealth lost 420,000 men, the United States, 292,000. In Poland six and a half million – one in five of the population – perished. Three and a half million of these were Jewish victims of the Holocaust.

INTERNET LINK

For a link to a website where you can listen to the announcement of the end of the war, and hear the reaction from King George VI and the crowds on the streets of London, go to **www.usborne-quicklinks.com**

THE AFTERMATH OF THE WAR

As summer 1945 turned to autumn, the victors were left with the difficult task of winning the peace. They needed to rebuild Europe and Japan, and establish stable new governments in place of the fallen dictatorships. But those responsible for plunging the world into war had to be punished first.

Hitler's deputy, Hermann Goering, listens attentively during his trial at Nuremberg. Sentenced to death by hanging, Goering committed suicide by taking poison on the night of the execution.

The war trials at Nuremberg

In the 12 months following the war, top German and Japanese politicians and generals were put on trial for war crimes. In Germany, the location was Nuremberg - a city closely associated with great Nazi rallies. Death sentences were handed down to the worst offenders. Those hanged at Nuremberg had their bodies burned in the crematorium of infamous Dachau concentration camp, and their ashes scattered in a nearby river.

Slow recovery

As well as claiming millions of lives, the war had destroyed millions of homes, bridges, railway lines, hospitals, factories and offices. In the "scorched earth" fighting of the Eastern Front, the Soviet Union lost a quarter of all its buildings, and 60% of its farm produce. Germany, too, suffered similar destruction. Other countries, though, had grown richer - especially the United States, which had provided so many of the weapons used to win the war. Canada, Australia and New Zealand - like the USA, untouched by bombing - also prospered.

Europe and Japan were hardest hit. The summer of 1945 also brought a drought which worsened already serious food shortages by causing a disastrous grain harvest. In Britain, bread was rationed for the first time, to make sure there was enough to feed the starving people of Germany.

Germany's fate

The First World War had ended with the vengeful Treaty of Versailles, which punished Germany severely. This bred a fierce resentment among the German people, which contributed to the rise of Hitler and led directly to the Second World War. Now, at the end of that war, the Allies were divided over the best way to treat the defeated German nation.

The Soviets wanted to strip Germany of its industry, and ship out factory machinery to help rebuild their own country. Before the war ended, US Treasury Secretary Henry Morgenthau proposed to turn Germany into a pre-industrial society, by demolishing its factories and flooding its mines. Such drastic measures would, it was hoped, prevent the country from ever being strong enough to go to war again. Fortunately though, other, more humane policies were adopted.

Rebuilding shattered economies

Britain and the United States realized, however, that the defeated nations needed to be nurtured as well as punished, to avoid another disastrous conflict in the future. In 1948, American Secretary of State George Marshall introduced the Marshall Plan, which offered economic aid to all European countries - regardless of which side they had been on. The Soviets refused to allow the countries they had occupied in Eastern Europe to receive this aid. But it played a vital role in helping the Western European countries, including Germany, to rebuild their shattered economies.

German civilians wait in line for soup rations in the ruins of Hamburg, a year after the war in Europe had ended.

From poverty to riches

Japan, too, suffered terribly after the war ended. Some people had to wear paper clothes and eat edible weeds just to survive. US General Douglas MacArthur was put in charge of ensuring that Japan became a stable and democratic society. He was extremely successful. By the time he left in 1951, he had introduced a new constitution, giving all adults the right to vote. He had also created the foundations that would enable Japan to become one of the world's most successful economies in the second half of the 20th century.

INTERNET LINK
For links to websites where you can watch video clips and see photographs of the war crimes' trials, and hear radio broadcasts from postwar America, go to **www.usborne-quicklinks.com**

THE WAR AND THE 20TH CENTURY

In scope and destruction, the Second World War was the most momentous event of the 20th century. In the last 2,000 years, only the Black Death in the Middle Ages had a more disastrous impact on the lives of those who lived or died through it. The shadow of the war haunted the rest of the century, and its effect on the world is still with us today.

Empires rise and fall

Before the war, Britain, France, Germany and Japan had all been world class military powers. Now they were eclipsed by the United States and Soviet Union - the world's two new superpowers. In the years after the war, Britain and France slowly came to terms with their status as second division powers, and gave up control over their once mighty global empires. This process of "decolonialization" created scores of newly independent nations.

New enemies, new friends

The Nazis had always known their opponents were political opposites, and had hoped that the communist Soviet Union would fall out with its democratic British and American allies. As the world began to recover from the conflict, the Allies' alliance did crack, and a "Cold War" broke out that would last for the next 45 years.

Redrawing the map

Soviet troops remained in Eastern Europe, and totalitarian communist regimes similar to the Soviet one were introduced throughout the region. Germany and its capital, Berlin, were divided into two - with the West under the control of the United States, Britain and France, and the East under Soviet control. In 1961, the East Germans built the Berlin Wall, to stop their citizens from escaping to the West, where they hoped for a better life.

INTERNET LINK
For a link to a website where you can explore the history of the Berlin Wall, go to **www.usborne-quicklinks.com**

Global hostilities

During the new Cold War, both the Soviets and Americans sought support from other nations. US troops were sent to Korea and Vietnam to prevent communist forces from taking over these countries. They succeeded in Korea, which is still divided into a communist North and capitalist, democratic South. But they failed in Vietnam. American fear of communism saw US troops based in Western Europe for the rest of the century.

The collapse of communism

The war gave the Soviet Union an opportunity to control Eastern Europe, and establish itself as the world's second most powerful nation. Only in the late 1980s, when the Soviet government tried to reform the communist system, did the Soviet Union collapse and give up its hold over Eastern Europe. For some, this meant freedom and the prospect of greater prosperity. Germany was reunited, and the hated Berlin Wall was destroyed. But for others, especially in Yugolsavia, which was ethnically divided, the communist collapse brought civil war.

After the Holocaust

After the war, many Jews who had survived the Holocaust joined others in Palestine, then under British control. When the British left in 1948, Jews in Palestine established the state of Israel. War broke out between Israel, the Palestinians and the surrounding Arab nations, which has continued, on and off, ever since. Israel has survived, not least because of massive help from the United States. The existence of Israel, and the refugee status of the Palestinians, has contributed directly to the rise of militant Islamic fundamentalism in recent times.

THE WAR ON FILM AND TV

The war remains a popular topic with both cinema and television audiences. Here are some productions that combine watchability with broad historical accuracy. All these are also available on video or DVD. Some feature harrowing depictions of violence which will not be suitable for younger viewers.

The Longest Day

directed by Ken Annakin, Andrew Marton and Bernhard Wicki, 1962

This spectacular and comprehensive depiction of the D-Day landings of June 6, 1944 was based on the Cornelius Ryan book of the same name. Unlike the more recent *Saving Private Ryan*, the film portrays events from the perspective of all the participants - British, American, Commonwealth, French and German.

Memphis Belle

directed by Michael Caton-Jones, 1990

Although it occasionally lapses into sentimentality and cliché, this depiction of the final mission of a US bomber crew based in England gives a strong impression of the everyday tensions and dangers of the air war over Europe. It is based closely on a true story.

Das Boot

directed by Wolfgang Petersen, 1981

This fascinating portrayal of the crew of a German U-boat during its final mission, shows the claustrophobic world of the submariner in all its grimy, terrifying detail.

Schindler's List

directed by Steven Spielberg, 1993

Based on Thomas Keneally's book *Schindler's Ark*, this tells the story of the Holocaust through the tale of German industrialist Oskar Schindler's attempts to save Jewish workers employed in his factory.

Enemy at the Gates

directed by Jean-Jacques Annaud, 2000

This account of the Battle of Stalingrad gives a good idea of the dreadful ordeal faced by both German and Soviet troops during this pivotal battle of the war.

Tora! Tora! Tora!

directed by Richard Fleischer, 1970

Taking its name from the Japanese radio codeword to signal that the attack had been a total surprise (*Tiger! Tiger! Tiger!*) the film captures the chaos of the day well. Although lacking the spectacular special effects of the more recent *Pearl Harbor* (2001), most critics agree that *Tora! Tora! Tora!* is a more accurate history.

Battle of Britain

directed by Guy Hamilton, 1969

An all-star cast reenacts the story of how Britain was defended by the Royal Air Force in the late summer of 1940.

Band of Brothers

directed by Phil Alden Robinson and Richard Loncraine, 2000

A scrupulously accurate dramatic recreation of the experiences of a group of American soldiers fighting from Normandy and into Germany during 1944 and 1945.

The World at War

directed by Jeremy Isaccs, 1973

With a poetic and mesmerizing narration by Laurence Olivier, and a haunting score by Carl Davis, this 32-part epic mixes contemporary newsreel film with interviews from surviving soldiers, politicians - and even Hitler's secretary.

The Nazis - A Warning from History

produced by Laurence Rees, 1997

This documentary series takes a fresh look at the Third Reich. Similar in style to the *World At War* in its mixture of archive footage and interviews with surviving eyewitnesses, the makers ask the ominous question, "Could it happen again?"

The War of the Century

produced by Laurence Rees, 1999

This series looks at the most fiercely fought and barbaric aspect of the war: the German invasion of the Soviet Union. The production makes fascinating use of recently released archive material, which had previously been forbidden to documentary makers by the Soviet Union.

Hell in the Pacific

produced by Jonathan Lewis, 1997

This four-part series covers the Pacific conflict from Pearl Harbor to Hiroshima and Nagasaki with first-hand accounts from participants. Lesser known areas of the war in the Pacific, such as Burma, are also covered.

INTERNET LINK
To see a longer list of films on the Second World War, go to **www.usborne-quicklinks.com**

GLOSSARY

This glossary explains some of the words you may come across when reading about the Second World War. If a word used in an entry has a separate entry of its own, it is shown in *italic* type.

aircraft carrier A large, long-decked warship from which aircraft can take off and land at sea.

Allies The nations that fought against the *Axis* during the Second World War. The main Allied countries were Great Britain and its empire, the Soviet Union, the United States of America and France.

armada A large number of ships or aircraft.

armaments The weapons and *munitions* used by a military force.

arsenal A stock of weapons and *munitions*.

artillery Large but transportable *armaments*, such as cannons and heavy guns.

Aryan A Nazi term for a "pure-blooded" German.

atomic bomb An explosive weapon that releases enormous energy by splitting elements such as uranium or plutonium. Also called an A-bomb.

Axis The pact signed between Germany, Italy and Japan, on September 27, 1940, joined by other, smaller nations - Slovakia, Rumania, Hungary, Croatia and Bulgaria - who opposed the *Allies* in the Second World War.

barrage balloon An elongated balloon tethered over a military target to support cables or netting that hinder low-flying enemy planes.

battleship A large heavily-armed and fortified warship.

blitzkrieg A fast-moving attack, using tanks, motorized troops and aircraft, used to great effect by the German army at the beginning of the Second World War. (The word means *lightning war* in German.)

bunker An underground defensive position or protective chamber.

censorship The control or suppression, often by a government, of information that threaten its goals.

civilian Anyone who is not a member of the armed forces.

colony A geographical area under the political control of another country.

commando A member of a small military unit specially trained to make quick, destructive raids by both land and sea in enemy territory.

Communism A political system in which the state controls the wealth and industry of a country on behalf of the people. People who follow this system are known as Communists.

comrade A fellow member of a group, especially a squad of soldiers, sailors or aircrew.

concentration camp A guarded prison camp where civilians and political prisoners are held during wartime, usually under harsh conditions.

conscription Compulsory recruitment of citizens into the armed forces.

convoy ships Merchant ships that travel in a group across a sea, with warships to protect them from attack.

cruiser A large warship that is faster than a *battleship* but has less fortification and firepower.

death camp A *concentration camp* where the captives are deliberately killed or worked to death.

democracy A political system in which the citizens can freely elect people to represent them.

deport To expel someone from a country.

destroyer A small warship that is easy to direct and position. It can be armed with guns, *torpedoes* and depth charges.

dictatorship A political system in which one ruler, usually known as a dictator, holds absolute power over their country or empire.

dive bomber A military aircraft that releases its bombs during a sharp dive towards its target, to improve the chances of an accurate hit.

dry dock A large, basin-shaped structure from which water can be drained, used for building or repairing a ship below its water line.

empire A group of countries or territories under the control of another country.

epidemic A widespread outbreak of a disease.

espionage The use of spies to obtain information, particularly political or military secrets.

evacuate To send troops or civilians away from a threatened area, for safety. During the Second World War, many civilians were evacuated from cities to rural areas.

evacuee Someone who has been evacuated.

exiled Sent away or banished from a country.

fascism A system of government usually run by a dictator, often characterized by extreme *nationalism*, in which opposition is suppressed by terror and *censorship*.

front line The boundary along which opposing armies face each other.

garrison A military base or fortification.

ghetto During the Second World War, this meant a densely populated, enclosed district of a city, such as the Warsaw Ghetto in Poland, set up by the Nazis to keep the Jewish population cordoned off from the "*Aryan*" districts.

glider An aircraft which has no independent power and is usually towed by another aircraft.

guerrilla force A group of independent, armed *resistance* fighters.

Holocaust The term given to the Nazis' systematic slaughter on a massive scale of European Jews and other groups during the Second World War.

incendiary bomb A bomb that is designed to burst into flame on impact.

inflation An ongoing rise in prices, combined with an ongoing decline in the purchasing power of money.

kamikaze A Japanese word meaning "divine wind" which referred to a plane loaded with explosives to be piloted in a suicide attack.

Luftwaffe The name of the German air force before and during the Second World War.

Maquis Mainly rural *guerrilla forces* of the French *resistance* movement during the Second World War. They were named after a French word for the type of scrubby vegetation in which they were reputed to hide.

marine A type of soldier who operates on land and sea.

Marine A member of the US Marine Corps, an American body of sea-going troops.

missile A weapon that is thrown or fired.

morale The collective spirit or confidence of a group of people, especially in the armed forces.

munitions Ammunition, such as bullets, bombs and *shells*.

napalm An explosive mixture of polystyrene, benzene and gasoline which burns fiercely.

nationalism The belief that nations benefit from acting independently, rather than in cooperation with other nations. Extreme nationalism results in the belief that one nation is superior to all others.

occupy To seize and take control of an area.

partisan A member of a *guerrilla force*.

pillbox A low-roofed concrete structure on which a machine gun or antitank gun is positioned.

propaganda Information that is systematically spread to promote or damage a political cause.

racism The belief that race is responsible for differences in ability and character and that a particular race is superior to others. Extreme hatred of another race is often a feature.

radar A system that uses radio waves to detect and determine the distance of airborne objects.

radiation Energy given off by atoms. With some materials, such as uranium and plutonium, this radiation can be harmful.

radioactivity The emission of *radiation* from atoms.

reconnaissance An exploration and inspection of an area to gather information.

Red Army The army of the Soviet Union.

reprisal An act of retaliation or revenge.

resistance Relating to secret organizations that fought to overthrow the enemy forces occupying their country, especially in France.

sabotage To damage or destroy property and utilities in order to hinder an enemy's progress.

seaboard Land bordering on the sea.

secret service A government agency engaged in intelligence-gathering activities.

shell A hollow missile containing explosives.

Slavs A race of people occupying large parts of Eastern and Northern Europe, including Bulgarians, Russians, Serbo-Croats, Poles and Czechs.

SS An elite unit of the Nazi party that served originally as Hitler's personal guard and as a special security force in Germany and the occupied countries. SS stands for the German word *Schutzstaffel*, which means "protection squad".

stormtrooper Originally a member of the Nazi Party Militia, the SA. (SA stands for *Sturmabteilung*, which means "assault unit" in German.) More widely, the term refers to highly mobile troops used in *Blitzkrieg* tactics.

torpedo A self-propelled, explosive device which travels though water and can be launched from a plane or ship.

Vichy France During the war, the part of France under the control of a government that cooperated with Germany.

warhead The front of a *missile* or *torpedo* that carries an explosive charge.

INDEX

ACKNOWLEDGEMENTS

Cover (t) © CORBIS, (ml) © Hulton-Deutsch Collection/CORBIS, (m) © Jacques Langevin/CORBIS SYGMA, (b) © Getty Images/Keystone; **Back cover** (t) © Getty Images/Keystone, (b) © Yevgeny Khaldei/CORBIS.

p1 Getty Images/Three Lions; **pp2–3** © Getty Images/Poinsett; **pp4–5** Leonard J. Le Rolland; **p7** (mr) © The Mariners' Museum/CORBIS, (tl) © Hulton-Deutsch Collection/CORBIS, (br) © National Archives of the United States of America; **p8** (tr) © Bettmann/CORBIS, (bl) © CORBIS; **p9** (tr) © Getty Images/Keystone, (br) © CORBIS; **pp10–11** Getty Images/Fox Photos; **p11** (tl) © Bettmann/CORBIS, (mr) © Getty Images/Keystone, (bm) © popperfoto.com; **p12** (tr) © Getty Images/MPI; **pp12–13** © Ewing Galloway/CORBIS; **pp14–15** © Getty Images/Keystone; **p15** (m) © CORBIS; **p16** (ml) © Getty Images/Topical Press; **pp16–17** © Getty Images/Three Lions; **pp18–19** © Getty Images/Hulton-Deutsch; **pp20–21** © Hulton-Deutsch Collection/CORBIS; **p20** (b) © Bettmann/CORBIS; **p22** (tr) © Getty Images/Time Life Pictures; **pp22–23** © Hulton-Deutsch Collection/CORBIS; **p23** (br) © CORBIS; **pp24–25** With permission from IWM, CH26; **p25** (t) © Bettmann/CORBIS, (mr) © Hulton-Deutsch Collection/CORBIS; **pp26–27** © Bettmann/CORBIS; **pp28–29** © Bettmann/CORBIS; **p30** (br) SV-Bilderdienst; **pp30–31** © CORBIS; **p31** (mr) © Bettmann/CORBIS; **pp32–33** © Novosti (London); **p32** (tr) © Associated Press; **pp34–35** © CORBIS; **p35** (mr) © CORBIS; **pp36–37** © Getty Images/Keystone; **pp38–39** © Getty Images/Hulton Archive; **p40** (bl) © Getty Images/Hulton Archive; **pp40–41** © Getty Images/Keystone; **p41** (tr) © Bettmann/CORBIS, (br) © Getty Images/Fox Photos; **pp42–43** © Getty Images/Hulton Archive; **p44** (tr) Jasenovac Research Institute; **pp44–45** © Bettmann/CORBIS; **pp46–47** © Getty Images/Keystone; **p47** (tr) © CORBIS, (mr) © Getty Images/Keystone; **p48** © Hulton-Deutsch Collection/CORBIS; **p49** (tl) © CORBIS, (tm) © Getty Images/MPI, (tr) Novosti (London); **pp50–51** © Yad Vashem Archive; **p51** © CORBIS; **p52** (tr) © Getty Images/AFP, (b) © Yad Vashem Archive; **p53** (ml) © Michael St. Maur Sheil/CORBIS, (r) © FotoWare a.s 1997–2003. All rights reserved.; **pp54–55** © CORBIS; **pp56–57** © Bettmann/CORBIS; **pp58–59** © Getty Images/Georgi Zelma/Slava Katamidze Collection; **pp60–61** © Getty Images/Hulton Archive; **p61** (tr) © Getty Images/G. Lipskerov/Slava Katamidze Collection; **p62** (bl) © Time Life, photo Charlie Brown; **p63** (bl) © Getty Images/Evening Standard, (br) © Getty Images/Hulton Archive; **pp64–65** © FotoWare a.s 1997–2003. All rights reserved.; **p65** (tm) © Getty Images/V. Kinelovsky/Slava Katamidze Collection; **pp66–67** © Bettmann/CORBIS; **p67** (tr) © Getty Images/Haywood Magee/Picture Post; **p68** (m) © Getty Images/Fox Photos; **pp68–69** © Getty Images/Keystone; **p69** (br) © Getty Images/Fox Photos; **pp70–71** (t) © Museum of Flight/CORBIS, (b) © The National Museum of the United States Air Force; **p72** (tr) © Naval Historical Foundation, Washington; **pp72–73** © Bettmann/CORBIS; **p74** (bl) © Bettmann/CORBIS, (tr) © 2001 Topham Picturepoint; **p75** (ml) With permission from IWM, GSA905-80, (r) With permission from IWM, HU86069; **pp76–77** © CORBIS; **p78** (tr) © MARY EVANS PICTURE LIBRARY; **pp78–79** (b) © Sovfoto; **pp80–81** © CORBIS; **p81** (tr) With permission from IWM, MH6094, (br) © CORBIS; **pp82–83** © CORBIS; **p84** (bl) © W. Eugene Smith/Magnum Photos; **pp84–85** © Bettmann/CORBIS; **p85** (mr) © Getty Images/Keystone; **pp86–87** © MARY EVANS PICTURE LIBRARY; **p88** (tr) © Bettmann/CORBIS; **pp88–89** With permission from IWM, CBRI 113SF2; **pp90–91** © CORBIS; **p91** © Cornell Capa Photo by Robert Capa 2001/Magnum Photos; **pp92–93** © Ullstein/SV-Bilderdeinst; **p93** (tl) © Bettman/CORBIS, (br) © Ullstein-Ullstein Bild; **p94** (tr) © Getty Images/Time Life Pictures; **pp94–95** (b) © Hulton-Deutsch Collection/CORBIS; **p95** (mr) © Henri Cartier-Bresson/Magnum Photos; **p96** (mr) With permission from IWM, A25174, (t) © Bettmann/CORBIS; **p97** (b) With permission from IWM, FLM1627; **p98** (b) © Getty Images/Keystone; **p99** (tr) © PETER NEWARK'S MILITARY PICTURES, (bm) © Bettmann/CORBIS; **p100** (b) © Getty Images/Keystone; **p101** © Getty Images/Hulton Archive; **pp102–103** Getty Images/Picture Post/Hulton Archive; **pp104–105** © CORBIS; **pp106–107** © Yevgeny Khaldei/CORBIS; **pp108–109** © CORBIS; **pp110–111** © CORBIS; **p111** (mr) © Bettmann/CORBIS; **p112** (tr) © CORBIS, (mr) © CORBIS; **pp112–113** © CORBIS; **p113** (mr) © Bettmann/CORBIS; **p114** (tr) © Bettmann/CORBIS; **pp114–115** © Hulton-Deutsch Collection/CORBIS; **pp116–117** © Bettmann/CORBIS; **pp118–119** © Getty Images/Picture Post/Hulton Archive; **p119** (mr) © Getty Images/Time Life Pictures; **pp120–121** © Yevgeny Khaldei/CORBIS; **p121** (mr) © Hulton-Deutsch Collection/CORBIS; **pp122–123** © CORBIS.

Half-title page: Under cover-fire from a two-man machine-gun team, Soviet soldiers advance on German positions over the flat landscape of the Russian steppe.
Title page: American troops march along the Champs Elysées, during a victory parade on August 29, 1944, to mark the liberation of Paris.

Picture research: Ruth King
Digital imaging: Keith Furnival
Maps: Leonard Le Rolland
Website adviser: Lisa Watts
Additional editorial contributions: Elizabeth Dalby and Sarah Khan

For more information about the Imperial War Museum,
go to www.iwm.org.uk

Every effort has been made to trace and acknowledge ownership of copyright. If any rights have been omitted, the publishers offer to rectify this in any future editions following notification.